GREG MADDUX

★

CAL RIPKEN, JR.

Also by East End Publishing, Ltd.

BASKETBALL SUPERSTARS ALBUM 1996
MICHAEL JORDAN * MAGIC JOHNSON
SHAQUILLE O'NEAL * LARRY JOHNSON
STEVE YOUNG * JERRY RICE
TROY AIKMAN * STEVE YOUNG
KEN GRIFFEY JR. * FRANK THOMAS
BARRY BONDS * ROBERTO ALOMAR
MARIO LEMIEUX
THE WORLD SERIES: THE GREAT CONTESTS
THE COMPLETE SUPER BOWL STORY GAMES I–XXVIII
MICHAEL JORDAN
SHAQUILLE O'NEAL
WAYNE GRETZKY

For more information on how to order these exciting sports books, see the back pages of this book.

All East End Publishing titles are available at special discounts for sales promotions, premiums, fund raising or educational use. For details, write or call: East End Publishing, 54 Alexander Drive, Syosset, NY 11791 (516) 364-6383.

GREG MADDUX

★

CAL RIPKEN, JR.

RICHARD J. BRENNER

EAST END PUBLISHING, LTD.
SYOSSET, NY

Like all my other books, this one is dedicated with love to my two wonderful children, Jason and Halle; and to all the children in the world, may you always play in happiness and help to build a world that is free from fear, hate, and bigotry of any type.

I also dedicate this book to the memory of John Lennon and Carl Berkowitz, a wonderful, loving man who I miss dearly. Pete Seeger and Arlo Guthrie, thanks for the songs and the stories.

I also want to respectfully and fondly acknowledge the research and editorial work of Tracey Dils that made the Cal Ripken section of this book possible.

I also want to thank Tony Inzerillo, Lisa James, Steve Lipsky, Jim Wasserman, and Carie and David Falco, thanks for helping me pull it all together.

Finally, I'd like to thank Pat Corbin and the rest of Scholastic Book Fair's buying committee for their continued support.

GREG MADDUX * CAL RIPKEN, JR.
First Printing January, 1996   ISBN: 0-943403-39-1

The cover photos were supplied by Tony Inzerillo.
Cover design by Jim Wasserman.
Copyright 1996 by Richard J. Brenner – East End Publishing, Ltd.

Cataloging-in-Publication Data

920   Brenner, Richard J. (Richard Jay), 1941-
BRE   Greg Maddux * Cal Ripken, Jr. / Richard J. Brenner. - Syosset,
NY: East End Publishing, Ltd., 1995

     96 pp: ill.,photos; cm.
     Includes bibliography.

     Summary: A dual biography of two of baseball's superstars - four-time
Cy Young Award-winning pitcher Greg Maddux and phenomenal shortstop
and two-time American League MVP Cal Ripken, Jr.

     ISBN: 0-943403-39-1

     1. Maddux, Greg, 1966-   2. Ripken, Cal, 1960-
     3. Pitchers (Baseball) - United States - Biography
     4. Shortstop (Baseball)   5. Baseball players -
     United States - Biography   I. Title

     920; B; 796.357
     dc20

Provided in cooperation with Unique Books, Inc.

This book is published by East End Publishing, Ltd., 54 Alexander Drive, Syosset, NY 11791.

**Mr. Brenner is also available to speak to student groups.
For details, contact East End Publishing, Ltd.,
54 Alexander Drive, Syosset, NY 11791, (516) 364-6383.**

Contents

GREG MADDUX

1. Something Special

[Author's Note: For a number of years, many Native American groups have been appealing to sports teams to not use Indian names like "Braves" or "Redskins," or logos such as the laughing Indian depicted on the uniform of the Cleveland baseball team.

In support of Native Americans who feel that nicknames such as the ones cited above are demeaning, I have declined to use them in this book.

If you share my feelings that those nicknames are disrespectful, you should write to the teams and to the Commissioner of Baseball. Those addresses appear on page 91 of this book.]

Greg Maddux was born April 14, 1966 in San Angelo, Texas. But the Maddux family didn't settle down permanently until Greg was 10 years old. Until then, Greg, his older brother, Mike, and his mother, Linda, kept moving following the Air Force career of Greg's dad, Dave, from San Angelo to Greensburg, Indiana, then onto Riverside, California, and then on across the Atlantic Ocean to Madrid, Spain.

It was while he was in Madrid that Greg first started playing organized baseball. He was only six years old at the time, and was supposed to play T-ball, but his dad was convinced that Greg could succeed in the Pee-Wee program against older children. Dave's persistence paid off, but only after he had agreed to become the coach of Greg's Pee-Wee team.

It was at that point that Greg became used to competing against older and bigger kids, even tagging along and being included in games with Mike and his friends, most of whom, like Mike, were five years older than Greg.

At first, Greg had to take a backseat when he played in those games. "In all the basketball and baseball games, I was always the last one picked," recalled Greg. "But that was to be expected."

Even back then, Dave was convinced that his younger son wouldn't be last in line for too long.

"I always knew Greg was something special. When Mike was 11, his friends would ask Greg to play, too, and that sent a message to me.

"He was always the littlest kid on the team and he had to play harder to succeed. But he was never intimidated by kids who were older or bigger than him. He's always been competitive in everything he does. We still play a lot of golf together. I used to beat him in everything, and now I can't beat him at anything."

Playing in games with older children helped Greg to develop his skills at a much quicker pace than he normally would have. "Then he'd go back and play with kids his age, and it was no contest. He was head-and-shoulders above the rest of them. Of course, when we were on the field together, he was always second-best to me," laughed Mike, who has always been more outgoing than Greg, who tends to be soft-spoken and reserved, especially with strangers.

When Greg was ten years old, his dad retired from the Air Force and the family settled in Las Vegas, where they all still live. And by the time Greg was 12, his ability as a pitcher was so advanced that it actually backfired against him.

"His Little League coach wouldn't let him pitch," remembers Mike, "because he thought it was unfair to the other teams. Nobody could hit him. It wasn't fun for anybody. You've got to respect the coach's decision, because he was out to make the game fun."

Greg eventually moved on to Valley High School, where his education as a baseball player was accelerated by Roger Fairless, who was considered to be one of the finest high school coaches in the country.

"Roger was a big influence," acknowledged Greg. "I think I learned from him how important work habits are. We were

10

always reminded how to react to certain situations, like when to cover first base, things like that.

"I took that for granted until I signed with the Cubs and went to rookie ball. We had guys there who had *no* idea how to cover first. I just assumed everybody was getting that type of coaching. He actually taught me a lot of the fundamentals that are used up here in the big leagues."

Fairless, who now coaches at Green Valley High School, teaches the game from the bottom up, breaking baseball down to its basics, and then constantly drilling his players in those ABCs. Although the drill work can seem tedious while it's being practiced over and over again, Fairless's methods have produced big paybacks, including nine Nevada State Championships.

The program devised by Fairless certainly proved to be a big plus for Greg, who made All-State in his junior year, after leading Valley to the state finals. Greg, according to Fairless, had pitched too recently to start the championship game, but the coach did call on his ace in the final inning with Valley leading 5–3. However, Greg gave his coach and teammates a large dose of the willies by walking the first three batters he faced. Greg, though, made up for his unusual lack of control by proceeding to strike out the next three batters, earning the save that brought Valley the Nevada State Championship.

Although Greg wasn't an outstanding hitter, he was such a superb athlete that during his senior season Fairless often had Greg patrolling center field when he didn't have him toeing rubber on the mound.

It was as a pitcher, though, that Greg showed that he was something special, and earned his second successive All-State award.

"He threw in the mid-80s," remembers Fairless in talking about the miles-per-hour speed on Greg's fastball. "We've had guys in the 90s, but the thing that always made Greg different was his control and poise on the mound.

"He almost never got behind in the count or got in trouble, and his fastball always had good movement. And he pitched in the same aggressive manner no matter which team we were playing or what the score was.

"Plus, Greg was always first and foremost a team player and never had an attitude or acted as if he were a star."

Greg's pitching skills and positive personality naturally drew the intense interest of college scouts, and Greg did come close to accepting a scholarship offer from the University of Arizona. But after he was selected in the second round of the 1984 June free-agent draft by the Chicago Cubs, Greg decided to turn pro.

"I was only going to college to play baseball anyway, and the Cubs were offering $80,000. It was hard to turn down."

2. Climbing the Ladder

Greg's first step up the ladder to the major leagues started in Pikeville, Kentucky, in the rookie Appalachian League. But before Greg threw his first pitch as a pro, he made the very mature decision to put his bonus money in the bank and keep it there until he reached the big leagues.

Greg had begun learning the value of money when he had earned $3.50 per hour loading and unloading trucks at a Las Vegas department store while he was still attending high school. And while he had confidence in his abilities, Greg was also realistic enough to know that only a tiny fraction of the players who get drafted ever make it to the majors. And he was also aware of the fearful fact that any professional athlete is only one serious injury away from becoming an unemployed person.

Greg stuck with his decision to leave the bonus money in the bank despite the fact that he earned only $424.00 per month while he was pitching at Pikeville. "I always had enough to get by," shrugged Greg. "I wanted to hold on to the bonus money in case of an emergency, or to fall back on for my education if I had to."

Greg, though, experienced a rapid rise through the Cubs' minor league system, starting with a 6–2 record that first season in Pikeville, followed by a 13–9 record at Peoria in 1985. Then in 1986, Greg raced up the final three rungs of the ladder as if he had a rocket in his pocket, starting the season at the Cub's Class AA team in Pittsfield, Massachussetts, and finishing it in Chicago's Wrigley Field.

It was in Pittsfield that Greg first teamed up with Dick Pole, a pitching coach who wound up having an important and lasting impact on Greg's career. Until he met Pole, Greg had been able to succeed on sound techniques and raw ability, without ever thinking all that much about the art of pitching or his own particular talents.

13

"Dick helped me to learn about myself as a pitcher," explained Greg. "He made me realize that not everybody can pitch the same way. You have to find a way that works for you, then try to improve off that and go from there."

Pole's persuasiveness helped Greg to post a 4–3 record and a 2.69 earned run average in Greg's eight-game stay in Pittsfield. That performance propelled him up to Class AAA Iowa, where he racked up a 10–1 record and earned a quick ticket to the top rung of the ladder, the Big Show.

Greg kicked off his big league career with an 11–3 win over the Reds in Cincinnati, and he also pitched the Cubs to an 8–3 victory over big brother Mike, who was pitching for the Philadelphia Phillies at the time. "The last time I faced him, I think, was in the backyard playing wiffle-ball," said Mike. "I think we both hit about .700."

Prior to taking an early shower, Mike managed to touch Greg for a base hit on a Baltimore chop over third base, so the little brother breathed a big sigh of relief when he reached Mike for a single to left. "I had to get a hit or hear about his 18-hopper all winter," smiled Greg, who was the youngest player in the majors, and who had such a baby face that Gene Michael, the Cubs' manager at the time, nicknamed him "Batboy."

Although Greg lost his other four starts, he had made an amazingly quick trip to Chicago, and both he and the team were looking forward to an even bigger year in 1987.

3. Turnaround

The new year got off to a happy beginning for Greg when he married Kathy Onnowon, who had been earning her college degree in business management at the University of Nevada–Las Vegas while Greg had been pitching his way to Wrigley Field.

Greg, who is an avid golfer, began the big day by playing a round of golf with some of his buddies. When Greg isn't competing on a baseball diamond, a golf course, or over a game of Nintendo, he tends to be a relaxed and laid-back type of person, so it wasn't surprising when he spoke about the schedule for his wedding day by saying, "Tee up at 8:30 a.m., put on the tux at 1, and say, 'I do' at 5."

Greg also started the 1987 season in pleasing fashion by winning three of his first four decisions. But by the tail end of August his record had bottomed out at 6–14, including six straight losses, while his ERA had ballooned to 5.61.

"I had gotten into a lot of bad habits. I was used to getting guys out with the fastball in the minors, but you can't rely on just that in the majors," explained Greg, whose confidence was shaken by his losing streak.

"I threw fastball after fastball and couldn't get people out," recalled Greg. "There was always one thing or another weighing on my mind. I was always thinking, 'What do I have to do to win? What do I have to do to turn it around?'

"I thought my stuff was as good as guys who were winning, but after a while you begin to doubt yourself."

Greg's losing certainly hadn't stemmed from a lack of trying. "From what I've seen, the kid's never going to be satisfied," said John Vukovich, who was Chicago's third-base coach. "That's a quality we hope to find in a young player, the desire to get better." Vukovich also admired Greg's aggressiveness, even as a base runner. "I sent him in from second on a single to left, and he should have been out by 20 to 30 feet. But you never know what's going to happen. Sure enough, Greg barrels over [San Diego Padres' catcher Benito] Santiago. And Santiago bobbled the ball. You don't often see a pitcher run the bases like that."

Greg's losing could, however, be traced to an overreliance on a fastball that wasn't any more than average for a major league pitcher—as well as, perhaps, an unwillingness to follow the suggestions of Herm Starrette, who was the Cubs' pitching coach.

"The kid's stubborn. We talk to him but he doesn't always listen. There are certain things we know about certain hitters and we try to pound what we know into his head. But he doesn't always take our word for things, and he's reluctant to change."

Greg's late-season slide earned him a return ticket to Iowa, where he went 3–1 under the careful gaze of Dick Pole, who had been promoted to Triple-A.

Greg, though, was anxious to convince himself that he could become a consistent winner in the big leagues. "I had already proved myself in Triple-A. The next step was to prove myself in the majors, but it was a struggle."

He knew that he had a lot of work to do to achieve his goal, so he packed his bags and spent the offseason playing for Maracaiboin in the Venezuelan Winter League, where he worked with Dick Pole, his pitching guru.

Pole was able to persuade his star pupil to stop trying to overthrow his fastball, which only flattened it out and took away the movement that made it an effective pitch. Pole also helped Greg gain the confidence to rely on his curve and his changeup when he got behind in the count, so that hitters couldn't sit on his heater. And he also got Greg to concentrate on keeping the ball low in the strike zone while moving it from corner to corner to further keep batters off balance.

"The way Greg responded to getting sent back to Iowa tells you something about him," declared Pole. "He could have sat and moped, but he was there the next day wanting to get to work on improving his pitching. And that's the same attitude that he brought to Venezuela."

Despite Pole's advice and his own hard work, Greg went to spring training in 1988 thinking that he only had a 50–50 chance of making a Cubs staff that had been upgraded by trades and free-agent signings. But Greg's work with Pole wound up paying off like the top prize in the Illinois State Lottery by matching his preseason goal of 12 wins with a 3–0 whitewashing of the Montreal Expos on June 18. Five days later, Greg notched his 13th victory with a complete game win over the New York Mets, who were the top team in the National League East. "He has as much movement as I've ever seen on a fastball," marvelled Wally Backman, who was the Mets' second baseman. Typically, though, Greg downplayed his achievement, attributing his triumph to good breaks.

"That's the way he is," said Cubs pitcher Rick Sutcliffe. "He holds the Mets to one run and talks about how lucky he is. He's just a shy kid until he goes to the mound. Then he's got guts the size of a basketball."

Greg's five straight wins in June raised his record to 13–3 and lowered his ERA to 2.14 while earning him NL Pitcher of the Month honors. Then he won his next two decisions, running his winning streak to nine games and taking a major league best 15–3 record to the All-Star Game.

"He hasn't pitched a bad game," declared Don Zimmer, who had taken over as Cubs manager at the start of the season. "In fact, he's only pitched a few bad innings."

Greg realized that his hard work in the winter league with Dick Pole had helped him to progress towards becoming a big-time big league pitcher. "When I get into jams now, I try to think and pitch my way out of them instead of throw my way out like I did last year. That's the biggest difference and the reason for the turnaround. Last year, I had no idea what I was doing. I didn't know what I was throwing or where I was throwing it. I had only one real pitch, the fastball. The only reason I won *any* games is because I started 27 times."

But after his nightmarish experience the previous season, Greg wasn't about to allow his sudden dream-like success to go to his head. "I know that if you let down, it can turn like that," he said with a snap of his fingers.

And, in fact, the second half of the season did turn into a mini-meltdown for Greg, who went 3–5 with a 4.92 ERA after the All-Star break. Most people in the Chicago organization, including Dick Pole, who was now the Chicago pitching coach, thought that Greg had simply worn down. Greg was willing to admit that he had lost a little of his fastball as the season progressed, but he adamantly refused to offer an alibi for his second-half fall-off. "I didn't think I was tired. I think that was an excuse that everyone made for me," said Greg, ignoring the fact that he had pitched almost nonstop for a year-and-a-half, and who at the time weighed only 150 pounds.

Actually, Greg didn't need any alibi for a season in which he had finished among the NL leaders in wins, winning percentage, complete games, innings pitched, and ERA, while establishing himself as a front-line major league pitcher. As Don Zimmer pointed out, "I don't think the world can expect a 22-year-old kid to pitch flawlessly for five straight months."

4. Little Things Add Up

Although Greg wouldn't blame his poor second-half performance on arm fatigue, he did decide to spend the winter at home in Las Vegas. "I won't pick up a ball until after the new year. I'll lift weights, and then after the holidays I'll start throwing."

Despite the winter's rest, Greg struggled with an 0–3 record at the start of the 1989 season. But then he turned himself around to finish at 19–12, with a 2.95 ERA, while helping the Cubs charge to the top of the NL East. "When we had a shot at winning the division, he turned it on like the best pitchers in baseball do," declared 16-game winner Rick Sutcliffe. "He gave us the opportunity to win it."

Greg also showed that he was first of all a team player by declining the opportunity to go for his 20th win on the final Saturday of the season, preferring instead to be well-rested for the beginning of the National League Championship Series against the San Francisco Giants.

Unfortunately for Greg and the Cubs, the extra days off didn't do any good as Will Clark clubbed Greg for a double and a pair of home runs, including a fourth-inning grand slam, that sparked the Giants to an 11–3 win in the first game of the NLCS. Greg was also hit hard in his second start, in Game 4, surrendering four runs in 3 1/3 innings as the Cubs went on to lose the game and then the series, 4 games to 1.

"That was the most disappointing time of my career because we had an opportunity to go to the World Series and I didn't pitch very well," recalled Greg afterwards. "I'd like to get back there again to see if I learned anything."

Although Greg had been ground up by the Giants, there was no mistaking the fact that he was on his way to becoming one of baseball's top stars. One sign of that status was his third place finish in the voting for the 1989 NL Cy Young Award, which is given annually to the league's top pitcher. Then there was his total of 37 wins over the previous two years, a number matched by only four other big leaguers during the 1988–1989 seasons: Dave Stewart (42); Orel Hershiser (38); Bret Saberhagen and Frank Viola (37 each).

Greg, though, tried to downplay the comparisons between himself and the game's veteran hurlers. "I've pitched well for two years; those guys pitched well for six or seven seasons."

Manager Don Zimmer, however, had a different take on the situation. "He may be young, but he's one of the best pitchers in the game. You don't win 37 games over the past two seasons by mistake."

Over the course of the next two seasons, however, Greg's career seemed to level off in some respects, as his victory count feel and his ERA rose from their 1989 levels. He started the 1990 season strongly enough, winning four of five decisions, and also established a major league record for pitchers by recording seven putouts at first base in a 4–0 shutout over the Los Angeles Dodgers. "He's the best I've ever played with, as far as getting over to cover the bag," declared Mark Grace, the Cubs first baseman.

But then Greg became bogged down in an eight-game losing streak. Part of the problem may have stemmed from the fact that Greg didn't accept some advice from his pitching mentor, Dick Pole. "Just because I've hit a bad patch doesn't mean I have to change the way I pitch," said Greg. Instead of banging locker room doors or kicking the water cooler, Greg was smart enough to seek some help in the form of a sports psychologist.

"I was 4–9 and looking for reasons why. I knew I didn't have a physical problem and my mechanics were fine. The few hours' time I spent with the psychologist helped me on the mound and in my life. It helped my marriage and even my golf game. I learned to handle the wins and losses better. You know, even in the games you win, you need to understand the mistakes you made, just like when you lose."

After his sessions with the psychologist Greg proceeded to reel off five straight victories, win Pitcher of the Week honors and finish the season with a 15–15 record. Throughout the trying season, Greg did prove that win or lose he was going to continue to take his turn on the mound by tying for the league lead in games started and finishing second in innings pitched. He also staked his claim to being the NL's top fielding pitcher by perfectly handling a league-leading 94 chances and becoming the first Cubs pitcher to ever win a Gold Glove, an award that is voted for by the league's managers and coaches.

In many ways, the 1991 season was a carbon copy of 1990, minus the long losing streak, except that Greg hit his first major league home run and received a hefty salary increase, from $437,500 to $2.4 million.

Greg began the season by splitting his first dozen decisions, then closed with a rush to finish at 15–11. He once again demonstrated his durability by leading the NL in starts and innings pitched, while finishing fourth in complete games and second in strikeouts. Greg also earned another Pitcher of the Week award and his second successive Gold Glove, after leading major league pitchers in total chances and putouts.

After two seasons of moderate success that were more noteworthy for highlighting his work habits and his great glove work than for any pitching brilliance, Greg suddenly emerged as one of baseball's best pitchers in 1992. Although Greg's record was only a lackluster 10–8 at midseason, he had pitched so well that he was named to the NL All-Star squad for the second time.

It was at this time that Greg took a huge risk by turning down an offer of a five-year contract extension that would have paid him $27.5 million. Greg didn't have any problem with the dollars, which would have made him the highest priced pitcher in the game, but he did object to the fact that Larry Himes, the Cubs general manager, had told him that he had only 24 hours to make a decision. "Things just didn't work out," said Greg. "I'd say I'm more disappointed than bitter. I thought we were going to get it done. It's a letdown, but on the other hand, I look forward to December when I can become a free agent. We'll just roll the dice and see what happens."

Shortly after Greg and the Cubs failed to reach an agreement, Oakland A's general manager Sandy Alderson said, "The only thing dumber than the offer was turning it down." It wouldn't take long for Alderson to be proven wrong on both counts.

Greg, though, was thoughtful enough to buy an insurance policy that would take care of himself and his family in case he were to get injured before he signed a new contract. "If I went and got hurt, money wouldn't be a problem. A lot of players get hurt and miss an entire season. And as much as we travel, a lot of things can happen, even when you're in a cab driving down the freeway. I'd like to see all young players, especially, take their first big league check and use it to buy themselves some insurance."

Then Greg went back to work and by mid-August he had raised his record to 15–10, equalling his victory total for each of the prior two seasons. Actually, Greg's pitching was a whole lot better than his record indicated, since most of his losses resulted from the Cubs hitters going into hibernation. In the ten losses that Greg got tagged with, Chicago had been shut out *seven* times while scoring a *total of only five runs*.

Greg, though, refused to whine about the lack of support he had received. "Yes, it's frustrating. But that has nothing to do with pitching. I'm not going to worry about getting shut out when I have to worry about getting hitters out. That's my job."

Then Greg finished the season in style by winning five of his final six decisions and becoming a 20-game winner for the first time in his career. Greg notched number 20 the tough way, by shutting out the Pittsburgh Pirates, who had just clinched their third consecutive NL East title. "He's an artist," noted Jim

Lefebvre, who had taken over as the Cubs manager before the start of the 1992 season. "He's the best in the National League, and one of the best pitchers I've seen in my 30 years of baseball."

The Baseball Writers Association of America seconded Lefebvre's opinion by selecting Greg as the NL's Cy Young Award Winner, the first time since 1976 that the award had been presented to a pitcher whose team had posted a losing-record. Greg, who won by a wide margin of points over runnerup Tom Glavine of Atlanta, had led the league in innings pitched, tied for first in starts and wins, finished second in opponents' batting average, wound up third in ERA and strikeouts, and came in tied for fourth in complete games.

Greg also claimed his third consecutive Gold Glove by once again leading all major league pitchers in both assists and putouts. Greg's fielding ability is based only in part on his athleticism; the other factor is his willingness to work on that tedious aspect of the game every year, starting in spring training. "I've seen too many pitchers not back up a base, and so the runner gets to walk home on a bad throw. And I've seen too many pitchers get a ball hit right back to them and throw the ball into the bullpen. And how many times have you seen a pitcher not cover first base in time, allowing the opposition an extra out?

"These things are important, but they're overlooked in spring training. Guys just go through the motions and somewhere down the road they suffer for it. Those are the types of things that over the course of a season can make the difference between a winning or a losing record."

He also showed that he was capable of handling the bat by leading the Cubs in sacrifice bunts, an ability which not only helps create scoring opportunities but also helps to keep a pitcher in the game. As Greg noted, "Little things add up."

5. Ticket To Ride

After the end of the 1992 season, Larry Himes made the resigning of Greg his top priority. "I want to get Maddux signed first," said Himes, who had a lot of positions to shore up after Chicago's fourth place finish in the NL East.

Greg, who had spent the previous five seasons establishing himself as one of the top pitchers in baseball, wasn't about to be hurried into making a hasty decision. Over the span of those five seasons, in which the Cubs had played over .500 ball only once, Greg had made more starts, thrown more innings, and won more games than any other pitcher in the Senior Circuit. He had further demonstrated his durability by never missing a start, and he had displayed his consistency by winning at least 15 games in each of those five seasons, a feat that had been matched by only one other pitcher, Boston Red Sox fireballer Roger Clemens. Greg's accomplishments, culminating in his Cy Young Award-winning season, had definitely put him in the driver's seat and he was determined to use that leverage to test his value as a free-agent.

That winter turned out to be one of the most exciting free-agent periods of alltime, with lots of big-name players changing teams. Barry Bonds, who had just completed a three-year stretch in which he won a pair of Most Valuable Player Awards while leading the Pirates to a trio of NL East titles, was the hot ticket as an everyday player. The San Francisco Giants, who were trying to create a championship team and generate fan excitement, stepped up to the plate with a six-year $43.75 million deal for Bonds that established a new benchmark for baseball salaries. David Cone and Jimmy Key, who had helped pitch the Blue Jays to the 1992 World Series left Toronto, as did Dave Winfield, who had delivered the Series-winning hit. Meanwhile, Paul Molitor, who had played in Milwaukee for 15 straight seasons, turned in his

Brewers uniform and moved to Toronto.

Just as Bonds had been the crown jewel of everyday players, Greg was the pitcher who topped every team's wish list. The New York Yankees made a bold move by offering Greg a five-year, $34 million offer that was designed to overwhelm him and blow all the other contenders out of the water. The deal got so close to getting done that Greg and his wife, Kathy, flew to New York to do some house hunting. But while they were flying back to Las Vegas, Greg called his agent, Scott Boras, and received the surprising news that Atlanta had suddenly entered the picture with a five-year $28 million offer.

After discussing the pros and cons of the two offers, Greg decided to sign with Atlanta. The news of Greg's decision was so devastating to Yankee general manager Gene Michaels that he immediately hopped a plane to Las Vegas in the vain hope of getting Greg to change his mind. "This one *hurts*," said Michaels, who had been Greg's first big league field manager. "He's the best one out there. Nothing bothers him and he's a good guy with a simple lifestyle. He loves to play baseball and to compete, and when he's not playing baseball, he's playing golf. I never thought I could say this, but he's a steal at $28 million. He's a steal."

Michaels wasn't the only person who realized what losing Greg meant. "I feel sorry for the Cubs' fans that he's gone," said Greg's former teammate Rick Sutcliffe, who had moved over to the Orioles. "Larry Himes said Jose Guzman and Greg Hibbard will replace Maddux. They can't do that on the field or in the clubhouse. That just won't happen.

"He was one of the best teammates I've ever had. He's a guy that will do whatever it takes to help his team win. He's never been a 'me' or an 'I' person. He could have won more Cy Youngs if he'd received a little more support.

"He's got a heart of gold and a wheelbarrow full of guts. He's not afraid of anything."

John Schuerholz, Atlanta's general manager, was delighted to be getting a pitcher with Greg's credentials and a person whose value system he admired. "In this day and age of the grab-as-much-money-as-you-can, greed and avarice syndrome that has infected sports, it is somewhat surprising and refreshing for a player to demonstrate his concerns for something other than money," said Schuerholz, whose words could be applied at least as equally to owners as they could to the players.

Actually, the only people who were surprised that Greg could turn his back on $6 million were the people who didn't know him very well. "Greg's never been driven by money," explained Kathy Maddux. "Simple things make him happy. His Nintendo, playing golf. He likes to have fun and joke around, and he isn't at all stuffy. Clothes aren't a big attraction for him, because he prefers to be comfortable and wear sweats rather than suits. He doesn't really care if other people don't like the way he dresses, and it's not important for him to have a Rolex or other fancy things.

"Greg never gets mad and he's not demanding. He never expects me to have dinner waiting on the table. If I cook, great, if not, we just go out. It's not a big deal to him."

What was important to Greg was that he play in a city that both he and Kathy liked, that the franchise had a first-rate front office that was well thought of by its players, and that the team had a chance to win a championship.

"I don't have a lot of toys and I don't want a lot of toys," said Greg in explaining why he had left $6 million sitting on the table. "But I set out with three goals that I wanted to attain in the big leagues: win 20 games in a season, which I've done; make $1 million, which I've done; and pitch in a World Series, which is still missing. I had my nose to the TV in October when my old Chicago teammate, Damon Berryhill, hit a home run for Atlanta against Toronto. That looked like fun. Lots of fun.

"To have a chance to play in the World Series, I don't think you can put a price tag on that. That's something only 50 people get to do each year. It's unique. I remember how it was when I was a junior in high school and our team won the state championship. I remember that game just as much as I remember pitching in the playoffs with the Cubs, or my first day in the big leagues, or pitching against my brother. You just can't buy that."

But there are some things that money can buy, and people who need some assistance, which is exactly why Greg and Kathy decided to start the nonprofit Greg Maddux Foundation.

"We pick small charities, where we'll see our contributions make an impact," said Greg. Funded in part by Maddux's off-the-field earnings, the foundation has donated to the Steel Pitts Home (a shelter for abused women in Atlanta), the Las Vegas Boys Club, and Family Rescue (a shelter for women in Chicago).

The Maddux Foundation also regularly donates complimentary baseball tickets to nonprofit, special interest groups in the Atlanta area. In 1995, groups that were guests of Greg's included: Gwinnett County Children's Shelter, Rockdale County Industrial Opportunities, Operation Dignity, Hands on Atlanta, Carrollton Housing Authority, and East Gadsden Boys and Girls Club.

6. Furious Finish

Greg had signed with Atlanta because they were the team that seemed to offer him the surest and shortest route to his goal of pitching in a World Series. They had come tantalizingly close to winning the Fall Classic in each of the previous two seasons, losing a seventh game, extra-inning thriller to the Minnesota Twins in 1991 before falling to the Blue Jays in a six-game set in 1992.

Atlanta had a solid lineup which included third baseman Terry Pendleton, the 1991 NL MVP and hitting leader; a pair of hard-hitting outfielders in Ron Gant and David Justice, who surrounded a speedy center field duo of Deion Sanders and Otis Nixon; as well as two top middle infielders, shortstop Jeff Blauser and second baseman Mark Lemke.

The team also had what many baseball people believed to be the finest group of starting pitchers in the game, even *before* they had signed Greg. The reigning ace of the staff was lefthander Tom Glavine, the 1991 Cy Young Award winner and the only hurler in the major leagues who had won 20 games in each of the past two seasons. Then there was John Smoltz, a hard-throwing righthander who had led the NL in strikeouts while winning a career-high 15 games and the NLCS MVP award in 1992. Young southpaw Steve Avery had won only 11 games in '92, but he had shown his capabilities the previous season when he had used his mitt-popping fastball and sharp-breaking curve to ring up 18 wins and capture the NLCS MVP award. Finally, there was Pete Smith, who had been called up to Atlanta from their Richmond farm team on August 2 of '92 and had contributed a perfect 7–0 record to the team's stretch run.

The mental makeup of the starting pitchers was as impressive as their physical abilities. While the addition of the current Cy Young Award winner might have been a cause for friction or jealousy on some staffs, the Atlanta starters greeted Greg warmly. Tom Glavine spoke about how having Greg added to the mix would probably push each of them perform at an even high level. "That's what had happened in '92," said Glavine, referring to the fact that from the end of May on, the starters turned in a 55–25 record. "Everybody in the rotation got hot and we were feeding off each other with each one doing his job and the next guy going out the following game and doing a little better. That's the type of staff we have. Nobody wants to go out there when we're on a roll and be the guy who derails it."

Steve Avery welcomed Greg by declaring, "He's the missing link that we've needed to win a world championship." There was no doubt that the addition of Greg had raised expectations to the rafters, with billboards in Atlanta promising "This is How the West Will Be Won." But this team, and especially the starting staff, had been assembled to do more than just win a third straight western division title. "The acquisition of Greg Maddux gives us the most formidable rotation in all of baseball," declared general manager John Schuerholz.

Before any of them had thrown the first pitch of the 1993 season, they were already nicknamed the "Fab Five" and were being compared to some of the top starting staffs of all time.

"You don't even dream of a rotation like this. No manager really had a right to since Earl Weaver and the Orioles staff," said Atlanta coach Pat Corrales, who was speaking of the 1971 Baltimore squad that was one of two major league teams to ever have four pitchers win 20 games or more in a single season.

It was difficult not to think in superlatives about Atlanta's starters, but Tom Glavine tried to put some reality into the daydreams. "Some people in Atlanta basically believe that we're not going to lose a game. We're not caught up in how many of us are going to win 20, or if we're the best pitching staff ever. We're caught up in wanting to win and getting back to the World Series."

Greg also tried to put a cautionary note on the elevated expectations. "It's hard not to be optimistic," conceded Greg. "But I think those comparisons are best left until after it's done. It will be nice to say this is what we did instead of saying this is what we can do."

Greg, however, helped fan the very flames of expectations that he had attempted to dampen by overcoming his pregame butterflies and pitching Atlanta to a 1–0 season-opening victory over the Cubs in Wrigley Field.

Greg went into a mild slide after that sensational beginning, and after 19 starts his record was a shaky 7–8, despite a solid 2.84 ERA. At this point, sports talk shows in Atlanta were filled with second-guessers questioning Atlanta's decision to sign Greg instead of Barry Bonds, who was having another MVP season while leading the Giants to the top of the NL West.

At the All-Star break only two-fifths of the Fab Five were pitching as promised. Glavine and Avery were sailing along while Smoltz was struggling and Smith was working his way out of the rotation.

The bright dreams of spring seemed about to wilt in the hot days of July as Atlanta fell 10 games behind the front-running Giants. But then John Schuerholz helped turn the tide of the season by picking the pockets of the San Diego Padres and obtaining heavy-hitting first baseman Fred McGriff, in one of the most lopsided trades in recent sports history.

McGriff helped to ignite the Atlanta offense while the team's top four starters caught fire at the same time. Atlanta set a remarkable pace over the next five weeks, but their 26–10 record was only able to snip 2 1/2 games off the Giants' lead. However, Greg and his teammates weren't about to wave a white flag. "I still feel like we're in the race," said Greg, as the two front runners were preparing to tangle six times in the next nine games. "We have to beat them four, or maybe even five, out of six."

That looked like a tall order since the Giants were the best hitting team in the league and had lost three games in a row only once during the season. But Atlanta took the first two games in San Francisco, and then Greg supplied the broom by pitching Atlanta to a 9–1 win.

"That's where it all started," recalled Greg. "The most important thing for me mentally was going to San Francisco for that series. We knew we needed a sweep. Personally, that was my biggest game of the year."

Six days later, Greg again silenced the Giants' big bats, while David Justice drove in four runs and Atlanta coasted to an 8–2 victory that sliced the Giants' lead to 3 1/2 games. Typically, Greg tried to deflect all the credit to his teammate by telling reporters, "Don't forget David's diving catch. He saved a run, maybe two or three. He turned around the game by himself." Greg, despite his modesty, was named Pitcher of the Month for August.

In the clubhouse before Greg's second big win over San Francisco, Greg had given some pointers to a college pitcher on how to throw breaking pitches. Then Greg had picked up his golf putter and tapped in some putts on the clubhouse putting green. "Not a bad life," quipped Greg, as though he wasn't about to pitch one of the biggest games of his career.

"With him, it's hard to tell whether it's his day to pitch, or his time to sleep," said Leo Mazzone, the Atlanta pitching coach. "But he's one of the most amazing people I've ever known and the best pitcher I've seen in a long time."

As the two teams stayed neck and neck and the pressure-packed race ran deep into September, Greg revelled in the challenge. "This is when it's fun. It's not like it was with all those losing seasons with the Cubs when we would be 20 games out and you can't wait for the season to be over so you can go home."

Then Greg took the mound against the Expos and picked up his 19th win, which was the franchise record-tying 98th win of the season for Atlanta. "No question, he's the best pitcher on the toughest staff in baseball," said losing pitcher Dennis Martinez. "He can be any kind of pitcher he needs to be," added Montreal manager Felipe Alou. "If he needs to strike you out, he can strike you out. If he needs a ground ball, he can get that."

Greg, wearing a "Furious Finish" T-shirt, picked up his 20th win on the next-to-last day of the season, beating the Colorado Rockies 10–1. It was Greg's eighth consecutive victory and kept them even with the Giants, who also won their 103rd game of that stomach-twisting season.

The following day, the last day of the regular season, Glavine picked up his 22nd win and then Atlanta finally won the NL West as the Dodgers went on to demolish the Giants, 12–1.

The team had finished their season with a 104–58 record, tops in baseball, and it had shown its character with a 54–19 finishing kick, the third best stretch run in major league history. The first four starters had wound up delivering as advertised, with a pair of 20-game winners followed by Avery, who had racked up 18 wins, and Smoltz, who had turned his season totally around, chipping in with 15 wins.

Before the team even had a chance to catch its breath and enjoy its awesome accomplishment in overtaking the Giants, it was time to square off against the NL East-winning Philadelphia Phillies, the highest scoring team in the Senior Circuit. Because the divisional race had gone down to the wire, Atlanta manager Bobby Cox was forced to juggle his pitching rotation and give the first game start to Avery. While the lefthander pitched well enough to come away with the win, Atlanta wound up losing the game, 4–3, in 10 innings.

Greg, who was up next, was anxious to even the series and to get another crack at pitching in an LCS. "There's no question I'm more confident now," said Greg, when asked to compare this start with the 1989 postseason pounding he had absorbed. "I know what to expect now. The last time I was probably too excited. I don't think I'll be as intense this time."

Then Atlanta helped pave the way for Greg by pummelling the Phils for an LCS-record 14 runs, and he held up his end by holding the Phillies to only five hits and two runs in seven innings of precision pitching. "Going up against him is always a problem," pointed out Phillie manager Jim Fregosi. "He's the best pitcher in the league, maybe in all of baseball."

Atlanta also turned on the power to take the third game, 9–2, but the scrappy Phils regrouped and won the next two games, which gave them a three games to two lead in the best-of-seven series.

Atlanta had its back to the wall, but that wasn't exactly unfamiliar territory for a team that had rallied from 10 games back to win its division on the final day of the season. What's more, Bobby Cox had his pair of aces to deal. With Greg lined up to pitch the sixth game and Tom Glavine waiting in the wings for the seventh game, the dynamic duo were ready to close out he NLCS the same way they had closed out the regular season.

But then Atlanta's season came to an unexpectedly sudden ending as the Phils racked Greg for six runs inside of six innings and won the game 6–3. Although some observers thought that Greg threw stiffly after he was struck in his right calf by a first-inning line-drive, Greg never tried to alibi by suggestions that his pitching had been affected by the incident. And we'll never really know if the outcome of the game would have been any different if Greg's calf hadn't been struck. Sometimes, even superstars lose games, even championship games.

In the locker room right after the game, John Schuerholz showed that Atlanta was a classy organization by going over to Greg, shaking has hand, and thanking him for his efforts. "You had a great year, pal. You've been everything we expected."

Despite Greg's failure in Game 6, and his disappointment in letting down his teammates and not reaching his goal of pitching in a World Series, there was no denying the fact that he had performed brilliantly during the regular season and especially in the stretch drive when he reeled off eight straight victories and won 13 of his last 15 decisions.

Greg had led the NL with a 2.36 ERA and also finished first in complete games and innings pitched, while finishing third in strikeouts, fourth in wins, and tied for fifth in holding opposing hitters to a .232 batting average. He had also led the league's pitchers in putouts for a fifth straight season, breaking the NL record of one Hall of Famer, Grover Cleveland (1914–17), and tying the major league mark of another Cooperstown inductee, Bob Feller (1948–49 and 1952–54).

So it didn't come as any great surprise when it was announced that Greg had won his fourth consecutive Gold Glove, been voted The Sporting News Pitcher of the Year, and won his second consecutive Cy Young Award, easily outdistancing runners-up Bill Swift and Tom Glavine, who had recorded his third straight 20-plus win season.

Greg joined Gaylord Perry as the second pitcher win the Cy Young Award for two different teams, but he became the only pitcher to turn the trick in consecutive years. "You change teams and you want to make a good impression. I think I've done that," said Greg, in something of an understatement.

Greg also became the fifth pitcher in history to win the award back-to-back and the first National Leaguer to do since Sandy Koufax was a repeat winner for the Dodgers in 1966. Maddux, though, refused all comparisons with the Hall of Famer. "I don't consider myself to be half the pitcher he was. I just love to pitch. I love the competition. I enjoy it, but I don't dwell too much on it."

7. Reaching the Goal

Atlanta had been the major league's winningest team during the previous three years, and most baseball observers also considered them to be the most talented team over that trio of seasons. But after a pair of World Series losses, followed by the LCS loss to the Phillies, people were starting to talk about Atlanta as baseball's version of the Buffalo Bills, the National Football League team that had lost a record-setting four consecutive Super Bowls, a month before the major league teams reassembled for their 1994 spring training sessions.

In order to avoid that type of stigma, John Schuerholz and Bobby Cox decided to fine-tune the team; some of their moves were by design, while other decisions were forced on them by circumstances beyond their control.

The most significant subtraction was left fielder Ron Gant, who had hammered 36 homers and bagged 117 RBIs in 1993. When Gant suffered a broken leg in an offseason dirt-bike accident, the team decided to release him. Then Chipper Jones, the hotshot rookie who was going to replace Gant, suffered a season-ending knee injury during spring training. Speedy free-agent center fielder Otis Nixon, thinking that the team was committed to playing Deion Sanders full time, had signed with the Boston Red Sox. Ironically, Schuerholz would find Sanders wanting and wound up trading him to the Cincinnati Reds in May for Roberto Kelly.

Also missing was the veteran catching duo of Damon Berryhill and Greg Olson, replaced by rookie Javier Lopez and Charlie O'Brien, who had come to the team from the Mets in a trade that sent pitcher Pete Smith to New York.

Atlanta also found itself shifted into the NL East—a long overdue geographical correction—after baseball decided to realign and, amoeba-like, split each league into three divisions.

The changes and distractions didn't seem to have any ill effect on the team, however, as they broke out of the starting gate with a 13–1 record that included an April 8 no-hitter by lefthander Kent Mercker, the new man in the team's starting rotation.

Greg also got off to a tremendous start, winning his first three decisions while allowing a ridiculously low 0.35 ERA.

"That was a *clinic*," said Giants announcer and former major league hurler Mike Krukow, after watching Greg give himself a birthday present by three-hitting San Francisco on April 14. "It was a guy at the top of his game and who is on the way to the Hall of Fame."

"He's the best pitcher I've ever seen," declared Bobby Cox. "He goes out to the mound with a report in his mind on every hitter, and he's never confused. Once the game starts, he knows exactly what he's doing."

The team was firing on all cylinders, with major contributions coming from Javier Lopez, the rookie catcher, and two rookie outfielders, Ryan Klesko, who had taken over for Ron Gant in left, and Tony Tarasco, who had taken up the slack when David Justice had to sit out some games with an injury. "It's just been good pitching and a lot of hitting from our young guys," explained Cox.

The team's super start had some players thinking ahead to the playoffs before the season was even a month old. "We don't feel there's any team that can catch us," said John Smoltz. "We don't think we're ever going to lose two games in a row."

Smoltz was wrong on both counts, and so was shortstop Jeff Blauser when he made a more reasonable prediction. "Pitching is the one thing that's going to be a constant."

Mercker did turn out to be a pleasant surprise, posting a 9–4 record in the strike-shortened season. But Glavine, Avery, and Smoltz all had subpar seasons, while the bullpen wound up saving only 26 games and blowing 13 other opportunities. Greg, however, continued his masterful pitching throughout the season, the single constant in an otherwise erratic rotation.

Interestingly, Greg wasn't thinking in season-long stretches, but rather game-by-game, even pitch-by-pitch. By comparison, after Tom Glavine had earned his 100th major league victory, he said that he was one-third of the way towards his goal of 300 wins. Meanwhile, Greg, who had 121 big league wins under his belt, including six in 1994, wasn't looking past his next start. "I've got to win seven before I can win 20. The same goes for 150, 200, 300—whatever the number is."

By the second week in June, Greg had raised his record to 10–2 with a 3–1 win over Houston in the Astrodome. "The way he works out of jams, he's a magician," marvelled losing pitcher Greg Swindel.

Greg, who had given up 11 hits, an unusually high number for him, had kept himself out of trouble by getting the Astros to ground into three double plays. "I'll take a win any way I can get it. That's what's great about Astroturf. You get a lot of double plays that wouldn't be double plays on grass," Greg said, making it sound as though the double plays were a matter of dumb luck rather than superior skill. Greg, who had also helped himself by not issuing a base-on-balls, is a big believer in throwing strikes and always trying to stay ahead of hitters.

"He can go strike one with the best of them," pointed out Bobby Cox. "That's a huge advantage if you can do that. You can talk about pitching mechanics all you want, but strike one is the first step to success." And once Greg goes up 0–2, he looks to put a hitter away, scoffing at the old baseball adage of "wasting" an 0–2 pitch by throwing it way out of the strike zone. "If you look at the percentages of what hitters hit on certain counts, you'll find that 0-2 is the lowest average for any count," explains Greg. "So why would you want to waste a pitch and go 1–2? The average only goes up for the hitter. Why put yourself in a hole? At 0–2, you're way ahead of the hitter, so my thinking is to make the best pitch you can."

"I've never been around a pitcher that thinks more about how to get a hitter out," said Atlanta pitching coach Leo Mazzone. "He likes to outfox hitters and he's always thinking of ways to improve himself. Even his work between starts is intense. Even if his location is a little off when's throwing on the sidelines, he's not happy about it. He's very serious about his work habits and he has an intelligent approach to everything he does. For example, when he first arrived in Atlanta, I noticed that he was throwing most of his practice pitches from the stretch position. When I asked him why, he told me, 'Because I'll need to make my best pitches with men on base.' He's got a great deal of natural talent, but a lot of thought goes into what he does out on the mound. He's a pitcher in the true sense of the word."

Expos' pitching coach Joe Kerrigan seconded Mazzone's opinion. "Maddux is simply on a higher plane when it comes to pitch selection I.Q. He's always a step ahead of the batter."

The June 12 win over the Astros had made Greg the major's first 10-game winner, and lowered his ERA to a microscopic level, prompting questions about another Cy Young Award. Greg, though, wasn't about to start daydreaming about the future. "It's been a good beginning, but the season isn't over. If you start thinking about the Cy Young Award, or 20 wins, or pitching in the World Series, you'll stop thinking about pitching. Sure, the award would be nice if it comes, but all I do is throw pitches; everything else is out of my control.

"You have to realize that all you're capable of controlling is throwing the pitch. *You* select the pitch you're going to throw. If, for example, you think the hitter is looking for a fastball, you throw a slider. Then you do the best you can to locate it where you want to.

"If the batter hits it hard, you try to determine why and correct it the next time. If you make your pitch, though, and the batter gets a bloop hit, you can't get upset. You try to understand why each batter got a hit or didn't and go from there. At times, there doesn't seem to be a reason, but usually there is one. It all comes down to execution."

Greg continued to execute with utter excellence even though it was becoming apparent that the inability of the owners and the players to decide on an equitable sharing of money and power was going to disrupt the season. "You've got to mess with your head a little bit, to convince yourself that these games count," said Greg after he had picked up his 15th win by pitching eight shutout innings in a three-hit, 2–1 win over the Central Divsion-leading Cincinnati Reds.

"That's what you call being in the right place at the wrong time," said Reds pitcher Jose Rijo. "You face Maddux, you have to count on being perfect. I made one mistake, the home run pitch to Justice. I was nearly perfect, but as usual, you have to be absolutely perfect to beat Maddux."

Then, on August 11, one day before big league baseball would close itself down until the following spring, Greg went out and executed another three-hit gem, as he shut out the hard-hitting Colorado Rockies to raise his record to 16–6 and to lower his ERA to 1.56, the third lowest earned run average recorded since 1919.

Even more astonishing than the number itself was the fact that Greg's ERA was 1.09 below the one recorded by Oakland A's pitcher Steve Ontiveros, who had posted the second-best ERA in the majors in 1994. That difference *shattered* the largest previous spread, which had occurred in 1968 when Bob Gibson's 1.12 beat out Luis Tiant's 1.60 by 0.48. Greg also set a second major league record because his ERA was 2.65 below the league average of 4.21, erasing the mark that Dazzy Vance had set in 1930 when his ERA was 2.36 below the league average.

What was, perhaps, most amazing about Greg's accomplishment was that he did it in a year when hitters ruled the roost and only five other major league pitchers had ERAs that even dipped below 3.00.

Greg, who became the first pitcher to win consecutive ERA titles since Tom Seaver did it with the Mets in 1970–71, also tied for the league lead in wins and shutouts. He soloed at the top of the league in innings pitched and his 10 complete games were more than any other NL *team*, except the Dodgers, who had 13. Greg also walked the fewest batters per 9.0 innings, held hitters to a league-low .207 batting average, while batting .222 himself, and led all NL pitchers in total chances to help earn him his fifth straight Gold Glove.

Greg's dominance was so complete that he became only the eighth pitcher in this century and the first since Sandy Koufax in 1966 to lead or tie for the league lead in wins, ERA, innings pitched, and complete games. His overwhelming performance enabled Greg to become the first pitcher in major league history to earn three consecutive Cy Young Awards. Greg, who became only the 10th player to win the award by a unanimous vote, joined a trio of pitchers, Sandy Koufax, Jim Palmer, and Roger Clemens, who had won the award three times, and left him one behind the career leader, lefthander Steve Carlton.

Greg still wasn't ready to put himself in a class with those pitchers, all of whom are Hall of Famers, except for the still-active Clemens. "I don't feel like I've pitched enough years to be considered in that company yet," said the ever modest Mr. Maddux. "I think it takes more than three or four good years to be remembered as one of the alltime greats. If I continue to pitch another six, seven, or eight years and continue to do well, I might say I belong in that class."

But even Greg couldn't help but be impressed with what he had done. "You always set goals, but to win the Cy Young Award, or three of them, is never really a goal. You try to set goals that are a little more attainable," admitted Greg. "And you always want to keep your ERA under 3.00. But under 2.00, you don't even think of those things."

Just when it seemed that Greg couldn't get any better, he did.

In a shortened 1995 season whose opening was delayed by the continuing owner/player conflict, Greg produced another superlative season, leading the league with 19 wins and only 2 losses, and the majors with a 1.63 ERA, making him the first major leaguer to have an ERA below 1.80 in consecutive seasons since Hall of Famer Walter Johnson did it in 1918–19. Greg also topped the league in complete games, while allowing the fewest walks per nine innings and becoming the first pitcher in major league history with 20 or more decisions to post a .900 winning percentage.

Greg's performance helped catapult Atlanta to first place in the NL East, which meant they faced the Colorado Rockies in the first round of the playoffs. Greg had his troubles with the potent Rockies' lineup, giving up three earned runs in a 5–4 Atlanta win in which he didn't get a decision. Then he came back in Game 4 to beat the Rockies 10–4, despite a less than commanding performance.

Atlanta went on to subdue the Rockies in the Divisional Series four games to two and then, surprisingly, swept Cincinnati, the Central Division Champions, 4–0 in the NLCS, as the Atlanta pitching staff combined for a 1.28 ERA. Greg did his part in regular-season style by limiting Cincinnati to one earned run in Game 3.

"I'm dumbfounded," said Reds shortstop and NL MVP Barry Larkin. "You can't pitch better than he did," declared Leo Mazzone.

The win over the Reds propelled Atlanta into the Fall Classic against Cleveland, the American League champions, allowing Greg to fulfill the third goal that he had set at the start of his big league career—to pitch in a World Series.

After Cal Ripken, Jr., threw out the ceremonial first ball in the Series opener, Greg pitched the greatest game of his career by holding baseball's best hitting team to two hits and two unearned runs as he outdueled Orel Hershiser and won the game

3–2. "The ball is there, and then it's not," said Cleveland catcher Sandy Alomar, Jr. "I've never seen anything like it."

"That was the best pitched game I've ever seen," said Cleveland catcher Buddy Bell, who was named the Detroit Tigers' manager after the Series. "I don't know how you can be more perfect."

When that comment was passed on to Leo Mazzone, he chuckled. "Tell Buddy that when you see 700 innings of Maddux, you see that a lot. You're at a loss for words. I don't know what to say anymore."

Even Greg voiced satisfaction with his overpowering performance. "That was my best game ever, everything considered," said Greg, who was so elated about winning his first World Series game that he tore the lineup card off the dugout wall as a memento for his dad, and retrieved the ball with which he recorded the last out to mark the time for himself, as well. "Tonight was fun."

Atlanta took two of the next three contests, so Greg got a chance to wrap up the Series by winning Game 5. Greg couldn't get the job done, losing 5–4, but then Tom Glavine pitched a masterful one-hitter over eight innings in Game 6. David Justice supplied the only run on a long home run, as Mark Wohlers closed the door on Cleveland and gave Atlanta the first World Series in its history.

Although Greg did not have a dominating postseason, that didn't take anything away from a regular-season performance that earned him his sixth successive Gold Glove and fourth consecutive Cy Young Award.

"If there's anyway to compare this one to the other three, this one has to be the most special because of the World Series," said Greg. "When you win the Cy Young, you're like the only guy who goes home happy. But when we won the World Series, it was more special to see all my teammates celebrating in the clubhouse."

After winning an unprecedented fourth Cy Young, Greg may finally be relenting in his refusal to consider himself among the game's alltime greats. "It's hard for me to say where I rank. My history of the game only goes back to 1987 or 1988. I wasn't really a big fan when I was growing up. I didn't become a true fan until eight or nine years ago."

Leo Mazzone, though, has no doubts that Greg already deserves to be considered among the top pitchers in baseball history. "You have to start thinking of him in historic ways. This is a guy who could have pitched successfully in any era. Even top-shelf guys on our staff, like Tom Glavine or Steve Avery, will come in after Greg has pitched and tell me he's in a league higher than anyone else. I think you're seeing one of the greatest of alltime."

"You just have to marvel at him," said Detroit general manager Randy Smith. "He's the best in the game, the best in a long time. And it doesn't look as though he's slowing down."

Greg, unlike most other great pitchers, does not have a dominant pitch that terrorizes hitters, like Randy Johnson's 98 m.p.h. fastball. But he does throw his five pitches with uncanny accuracy and uncommon movement while consistently changing speeds and varying his location.

But perhaps even more important than Greg's physical skills is the mental posture that he brings to the game. Twenty-four hundred years ago, a brilliant philosopher by the name of Plato lived in ancient Greece. Plato believed that somewhere, on a higher plane, there existed a perfect ideal of everything—an ideal that humans could strive for but never achieve.

Most people learn to settle for mediocrity in what they do. For a much smaller group, however, that quest for perfection becomes a consuming pursuit. Greg is one of those rare people who doesn't measure success in conventional ways—by wins and losses, awards, or money. For Greg Maddux, there is a perfect pitch to be thrown to each batter in a particular situation in terms of speed, location, and movement.

Every time that Greg takes the mound he measures his performance not in the larger terms of hits or runs allowed, or even in terms of victory or defeat, but in how close he came, pitch by pitch, to pitching that perfect Platonic game.

PHOTO SECTION

Greg Shutting Out the Dodgers in 1990.
AP/World Wide Photos

The "Fab Five": Glavine, Maddux, Smith, Smoltz, and Avery.

AP/World Wide Photos

Around Comes the Arm.
Photo by Tony Inzerillo

In Comes the Pitch.
Courtesy of Atlanta Baseball Team

The Best of All the Rest.
Courtesy of Atlanta Baseball Team

The Heart of the O's.
Courtesy of the Baltimore Orioles

Bill, Dad, and Cal.
AP/World Wide Photos

Cal Cracks the Game-Winner in 1991 All-Star Game.
AP/World Wide Photos

Cal Hoists His All-Star Trophy.
AP/World Wide Photos

The Iron Man.
AP/World Wide Photos

CAL RIPKEN, JR.

1. Born to Play Baseball

On August 24, 1960, Calvin Edward Ripken, Jr. was born in Havre de Grace, Maryland, to a family whose lives were, in almost every way, connected with baseball. In fact, when Cal, Jr. —the second child in the Ripken family—was born, Cal's father was miles away in Topeka, Kansas, playing catcher for a Baltimore Orioles farm club. Instead of passing out cigars, Cal's father was busy driving in the winning run for his team.

But it wasn't only Cal's father who demonstrated a talent with the bat. His mother, Violet Ripken, first attracted her future husband's attention when she played high school softball in Aberdeen, Maryland. And Cal's uncle, Bill, had been a minor league outfielder in the Dodgers organization.

But Cal's father never had a chance to make it to the big leagues because he suffered a career-ending shoulder injury the year Cal was born. Since he loved the game so much, though, he decided to stay in baseball and became a minor league manager.

Soon life in the Ripken family fell into a kind of a pattern that revolved entirely around the elder Cal's career. During the school year, Cal and his older sister, Ellen, and two younger brothers, Fred and Billy, stayed at home in Aberdeen with their mother. But during the summer, the whole family hit the road with their dad, moving to wherever he was managing a team.

It was hard for the Ripken kids to leave their friends every summer, but they made up for that by becoming pals with each other. Even though Cal used to fight with his brothers, he also spent hours playing games with them, many of which he made up.

And, of course, there was baseball.

Cal's parents didn't try to push him into the sport, but it was so much a part of their family's life that it would have been hard for him not to become involved with the game.

"Baseball was talked about in our household all the time,"

said Cal. Baseball stories even became part of the goodnight ritual. "If I couldn't sleep, if I'd had a nightmare or something, my dad would come into my bedroom and say, 'Let's think about you hitting a home run in the seventh game of the World Series…'"

One time, Cal even played baseball in his sleep. His parents heard a commotion coming from his room and found little Cal running around his bed as if he were running the bases. He told them later that he was dreaming that he had just hit a home run in the World Series!

For Cal, being on the road with his family meant that he got to watch his father coach young players. He hung out in the locker rooms and listened to everything his father said. He wore a miniature Orioles uniform and got tips from all of the players, too. For three summers in a row, Cal, Sr. coached a team in Asheville, North Carolina, and Cal followed him to the park every single day. "I'd watch those games intently," recalled Cal. "After the game, I'd start asking my dad questions. I always wanted to know why he did something. By the time I was ready to play, I knew the right way to do things. I knew the Orioles' way."

But even though Cal learned a lot about baseball from watching his father, Cal, Sr. didn't have much time to watch his son play Little League baseball. It was his mother who taught him many of the fundamentals of the game and spent hours cheering her son on during the games. One time, when Cal was 11, she was the only parent who braved 30-degree temperatures and high winds to watch her son play Little League ball.

"When I look back on it, I really have to tip my hat to my mom. She took me to all of my games, congratulated me if I did well, consoled me if I didn't," Cal said later.

Cal began his Little League career as a catcher in Asheville, but soon discovered that he liked pitching or playing in the outfield better. Even as a Little League player, Cal was extremely competitive. In 1973, he led his team all the way to the state championship. Although the team then went on to lose in the Southeastern Regionals in Florida, that brief taste of being a champion was one of the biggest thrills of Cal's early baseball career. A few years later, Cal led another championship team, this one from Putty Hill, Maryland, to the Mickey Mantle World Series in Sherman, Texas, where they dropped a best-of-three competition.

Baseball wasn't the only sport Cal excelled at. He was also a top-notch soccer player on a youth team his dad coached. Cal didn't take to school so quickly, though. In fact, when he was in first grade, he would run out of the classroom and head home every time the teacher turned her back. But he eventually became a good student, especially in math.

When Cal was 15, his father was moved up to coach the Baltimore Orioles, giving Cal the chance to learn the game from major league players. Cal was playing baseball at his high school in Aberdeen at the time, but after practice, he would go directly to Memorial Stadium, sometimes still wearing his high school uniform. On weekends, he and his brother Billy would head to the stadium early and shag flies with the team and even take batting practice from the Orioles' pitching coach. Cal also had the opportunity to pick up fielding tips from Orioles' shortstop Mark Belanger, a perennial Gold Glove winner, and to learn about pitching techniques from future Hall of Famer Jim Palmer.

"I was like a reporter," Ripken said later. "I would review the game charts and have all my questions ready. Why did this guy steal? Why didn't the catcher throw on this play? I would fire questions at my dad. He'd tell me why everything happened. I'd question the players the next day, too. Why did you do that? What were you thinking?"

Cal put all the information he got to good use. Although he was a skinny kid, just 5 feet and 128 pounds when he was a freshman, he soon became one of the most popular athletes at Aberdeen High School while playing both soccer and baseball.

It was unusual for a freshman to make the varsity baseball team, but that's where coach Don Morrison decided to put him. Cal played mostly at shortstop his freshman year, but batted under .200 for the season. His sophomore year, he didn't do much better at the plate, hitting just over .200.

Although his work in the field was A+, thanks in part to the coaching he received from Mark Belanger, Cal knew he would have to hit better if he wanted to play pro ball. When he got down about his weak work with the stick, Cal went to his father for advice.

"Every once in a while, I'd go to him for a confidence-builder," Ripken said. "But he wouldn't soft-soap me. He'd say, 'You're not hitting the ball the way you can.' Then he would end his lecture with two simple words, 'Keep battling.'"

And that's exactly what Cal did. By the time he was in the eleventh grade, he had grown to 6 feet and was stronger and faster. He became the team's number-one starting pitcher and co-captain. His control was nearly flawless and he rarely walked batters. When he wasn't pitching, he played shortstop. His hitting improved too, and he finished the season with a batting average just over .300. He was disappointed when his team failed to win the county playoffs, but he went into his senior year determined to make another run at a title.

Even then he had the attitude and work habits that would propel him to big-league stardom. Cal worked hard on his hitting and was always the first one on the field and the last one off. When asked to describe his star player, his high school coach replied with one word—"focused."

The following year, Cal had grown to 6-2. He was made team captain and, at an early team meeting, made a stirring speech in which he insisted that every player, including himself, had to play as hard as possible.

Cal's leadership set off the alarm, and, along with his outstanding play, helped the team go undefeated for the rest of the season. Cal pitched 60 innings and struck out 100 batters, while posting a 7–2 record and a microscopic 0.70 ERA. He also led the county in hitting, with a batting average of .492, and had 29 RBIs in only 20 games. Cal capped off his high school career by pitching a two-hitter and striking out 17, while leading Aberdeen to the 1978 Maryland Class A Baseball Championship Game.

And, best of all, during his final season, scouts from major-league teams, as well as several top colleges, were eyeing him with keen interest for soccer as well as baseball. According to the scouting report of the Texas Rangers, Cal was "built like and has Jim Palmer-like actions . . . pitches well . . . good poise and savvy."

Hard work, determination, and a drive to succeed were the qualities Cal demonstrated early in his career. Those were also the qualities that would help to make him a major league superstar.

2. A Major Force in the Minors

If Cal Ripken had had a choice, he would have wanted to be drafted by the Orioles. After all, the Baltimore team was like family to him. But the O's weren't the only team that was scouting him. In fact, he was near the top of the draft lists of many big-league teams—not as a shortstop, but as a pitcher.

In the end, though, the draft went in Cal's—and the Orioles' —direction. The Birds selected Cal in the third round of the 1978 draft. His dad was on a road trip with the Orioles in California when it happened, but quickly placed a call to his wife.

"Today, we've had a son drafted," he said.

Violet, who had never doubted her son's future in baseball, simply replied, "Oh, I've known it would happen for months."

A few weeks later, Cal was headed to Bluefield, West Virginia, the Orioles' rookie team in the Appalachian League.

Cal wasn't alone when he headed to Bluefield. Tim Norris, a Baltimore native, was at his side. Norris had played for Archbishop Curley High School and had also been drafted by the Orioles. The two quickly became close buddies, and roomed together in Ilee Short's Boardinghouse after they arrived in Bluefield.

But even his new friend couldn't help Cal adjust to life in Bluefield or in the minor leagues. Although Bluefield was only 400 miles away from Ripken's home in Aberdeen, it was worlds away from what his life had been like as a champion high school athlete. For one thing, the minor league facilities were quite a step down from those that Cal had grown accustomed to at Aberdeen High School. And the town itself—with just 16,000 inhabitants—was much smaller than Cal was accustomed to living in. But it wasn't just the town or the rickety minor league stadium that Cal had trouble adjusting to. What was harder for Cal to deal with was that he was only 17 and was living away from his family for the first time. And skillwise, it was a big step up from high school ball to even the low minors, where almost every player had been a prep school or college hotshot. To make matters worse, he was immediately given the starting shortstop spot, which made him even more nervous. Cal carried his concerns onto the field, causing him to make so many errors and to hit so badly that a lot of Bluefield fans wondered why he had been picked so high in the draft.

When the fans and even some of his own teammates began to joke about his playing ability, Cal was nearly crushed and began to question his potential. "After all those mistakes," he later admitted, "I was scared to death."

Fortunately, manager Wilbert Miner understood what Cal was going through. Better yet, he knew how to encourage Cal and to give him tips on how to play better. He helped Cal block out the premature criticism and concentrate on learning and improving. Soon, Cal settled down and started displaying his abilities—making plays that he had misplayed earlier, spraying hits around the field. He wound up finishing his first pro season with a respectable .264 average, with 24 RBIs in 63 games. The only shortcoming that Cal showed was a lack of power, as he failed to hit even one home run.

His improved play and his work during the winter in the Florida Instructional League earned Cal a promotion to the Orioles' Class A team in Miami the following year. It was there that Cal finally drilled his first pro dinger. The home run couldn't have come at a better time. There were two outs in the 12th inning when Cal drilled a line drive over the wall in left field to pull out a win for Miami.

There were other changes in Miami, too. When an injury sidelined Miami's regular third baseman, Cal shifted from shortstop to take over the hot corner. It was as a third baseman— a position that requires quick reflexes—that he worked at fine-tuning his fielding. In short order, Cal began making the diving stops and quick throws that rob opponents of hits and kill off rallies. Cal also showed that he was coming on as a hitter, averaging .303.

Cal's play earned him a late-season ticket to the O's AA team in Charlotte, North Carolina, in the Southern League. Cal also played at Charlotte in 1980, where he grew to his present height of 6-4 and bulked up to 205 pounds. The results were astonishing as Cal, who had hit only eight dingers in his pro career, smashed 25 homers, breaking the team's home run record. He also led the league in two-baggers, and was the league's top-fielding third baseman, on his way to being named to the Southern League's All-Star Team.

In 1981, Cal started the season at AAA Rochester, only one step away from the Big Show. During his first week, he cracked two homers, and in late April really put on a display by hammering three home runs in one game. By early August, Cal had ripped 23 home runs, drilled 31 doubles, and had driven in 75 runs in 114 games, prompting the Orioles to make the call that Cal had been dreaming about since he had been a little boy: "Pack your bags and report to Baltimore."

3. Big League Ball

Cal came up to the Orioles during an unusual season. The players, having been unable to reach a labor agreement with the owners, had gone on strike in June, which resulted in a 50-day break in regular-season play. When the labor strife was finally settled, it was decided that the teams that were leading their divisions before the strike would play off against the teams that posted the best post-strike records. The winners would then advance to the League Championship Series.

The Birds had finished the first part of the season in second place in the American League East Division, just behind the New York Yankees. To make the playoffs, they would have to finish first in their division, and with only 51 games left at that point, the Orioles' management felt that Cal might be able to give them the edge they needed to take that extra step.

Cal was thrilled to finally be playing in the majors, and he was also glad to be back with his dad, who was coaching third base for the Orioles. During homestands, the two of them rode back and forth to Memorial Stadium together just like when Cal was a boy.

Cal's big-league career started off on a high note when, after Baltimore manager Earl Weaver inserted him as a pinch runner, Cal raced home with the winning run in a game against the Kansas City Royals.

But that was one of the few bright spots for Cal, who didn't score another run and wound up with a .128 average with only five hits in 39 at-bats during the remainder of the 1981 season.

Although Cal got to fill in both at third and at short, where he spelled his old infield tutor, Mark Belanger, he spent most of the games sitting on the bench.

The lack of action gnawed away at Cal. "It was eating my insides out," he said. "That's what baseball's all about—playing every day... I want to do what I can while I can."

The Orioles had a good season that year, but it wasn't good enough. They didn't win the second half of the race, so there would be no playoff spot for the team in 1981.

During the winter, Cal didn't rest. Instead, he played for the Caguas Club in the Puerto Rican League, leading the league with 49 RBIs, and capturing the league's MVP Award as well.

When Cal reported to spring training in 1982 for his first official season as a rookie, he was ready for action. There had been some important changes on the Orioles. Mark Belanger had gone to the Dodgers as a free agent, and manager Earl Weaver had traded third baseman Doug DeCinces, clearing a spot for Cal in the lineup.

The revved-up rookie started the season with a blast. In Cal's first at-bat, he smashed a two-run homer off Royal's pitcher Dennis Leonard. Later in the game, he added a double and a single, as the Orioles romped, 13 to 5.

"That's when I really started to feel like a big-leaguer," said Cal.

But Cal's good feeling quickly faded as he fell into a deep slump, collecting only four hits in his next 55 at-bats. Cal admitted that he was allowing the pressure of playing in the big leagues to get to him. "Sometimes it all got to me—the triple-deck stadium, the media, the whole major-league atmosphere.... I got a big buildup in Baltimore. All of a sudden I started thinking they were expecting me to hit all those home runs."

It wasn't only Cal who was mired in a slump. Cal's early season doldrums was part of a teamwide nosedive that saw the O's lose nine straight games in May, and drop to last place in the AL East.

Lots of players offered Cal advice, and his best friend on the team, first baseman Eddie Murray, was always there with a word of encouragement. Perhaps most importantly, Earl Weaver stuck by Cal, even though he was getting pressure to sit the rookie down. But it was a tip from California Angels slugger and future Hall of Famer Reggie Jackson that seemed to really turn Cal around.

During a game in May, Reggie pulled Cal aside and spoke some simple words of wisdom that helped pull the rookie out of his slump.

"Just go out there and do what you can do. Just do what got you to the big leagues, and everything will take care of itself."

Cal knew from that moment on what he had to do—he had to go back to the basics and work on his technique. And once he began focusing on the basics, Cal was ready for a comeback.

The very next day, he got two hits against the Angels and a thumbs-up sign from Jackson.

Even though Cal didn't realize it at the time, he was about to start making history. On May 29, he was all suited up and ready to play the second game of a doubleheader against Toronto. But at the last minute, Earl Weaver replaced Cal with Floyd Rayford. It was the last game that Cal would ever sit out. The following game he began his incredible streak of consecutive games played that is still going strong.

A couple of days later, he started a game against Minnesota, but was taken out and replaced by a pinch hitter in the ninth inning. It was the last time until 1987 that he would even be taken out of a game.

Cal had finally settled in and by July was posting Rookie-of-the-Year-type numbers, when he received an unwelcome surprise as he entered the locker room before a game.

"Have you seen the lineup card?" asked infielder Len Sakata.

Cal shook his head.

"You're at shortstop."

Cal was shocked. Weaver had made the change and hadn't even told him. Though Cal *had* played shortstop, he felt comfortable playing third base. In fact, his idol had been Brooks Robinson, the Hall of Fame third baseman who had spent his entire career with Orioles.

The fans—and the rest of the Orioles' management staff - thought Weaver was making a large mistake. At 6-4, 205 pounds, Cal was thought to be too big to play shortstop. In fact, he is the tallest player ever to play the position on a regular basis.

But Weaver was determined. He told Cal not to be worried. "Field it smoothly. Throw it accurately. And if they beat it out, then it's a hit, not an error, and it won't bother me."

Weaver made another important change, too. He moved Cal up to the third spot in the batting order, putting him just in front of cleanup hitter Eddie Murray. The change meant that Cal would get to see more good pitches, since teams wouldn't want to walk him when he was going to be followed by one of the top run producers in the game.

The move by Weaver proved to be an inspired one as the Ripken-Murray twosome went on to become one of the most dangerous batting duos in baseball.

After Cal moved over to shortstop, the Birds went 56–35, the best record in the majors over that span. But their second-half surge still left the Birds one game short of the division-winning Milwaukee Brewers.

Cal, who played in 160 of the 162 games, hadn't allowed the midseason switch to shortstop throw him off his game. He had, in fact, done his best to bring the Birds back, leading all major league rookies in home runs (28), doubles, RBIs (93), total bases, games played, at-bats, and runs, and had tied for the top spot in game-winning RBIs (11).

So when the Rookie of the Year award was announced, it didn't come as any great surprise that Cal was the runaway winner.

Typically, though, Cal didn't take all the glory for himself.

"My manager and my teammates really deserve it," he said. "They stuck with me when I wasn't doing the job."

In 1983, his first full year as a shortstop, Cal quickly became one of the top infielders in the game. Although he was not as quick or as flashy as some other shortstops, he used his keen knowledge of the game and of opposing hitters to put himself in position to make all the plays that a shortstop needs to make. "I have never seen him make a mistake in judgment," said veteran manager Tony LaRussa. "Never."

Cal's sense of positioning and his acute instincts, coupled with a strong arm and quick release, regularly allowed him to turn potential hits into routine putouts. And his size and strength were a big plus offensively, allowing him to post the kind of power numbers that far surpassed those of most middle infielders.

Cal got off to such a fast start and stayed so hot that he earned a spot on the American League All-Star Team. It was a heady experience for a second-year player, being on the same field with some of the players who he used to root for from the stands. Cal's day was even made happier when the American League earned a victory for the first time since 1971.

The Orioles, meanwhile, led by the dynamic duo of Cal and Eddie, were having their best year ever. The Birds, playing under Joe Altobelli, who had replaced Earl Weaver as manager, were averaging nearly five runs a game, the best in the league. They skyrocketed to first place and held the spot for 115 days, never falling more than three games behind the pace.

When the Orioles did hit a bit of a slump in the beginning of August, Cal was there to make sure that it didn't turn into a devastating tailspin. After the O's lost seven straight games, and dropped into fourth place, Cal came to the team's rescue by cracking a two-run homer in the eighth inning that broke a tie and brought the Birds a victory over the Chicago White Sox. That win set the Orioles off on a tear in which they won 33 of their next 43 games and clinched the AL East title. During the stretch run, Cal hit 10 home runs, notched 30 RBIs, and scored 42 runs.

Although they lost the opener of the American League Championship Series against the White Sox, they went on to win the next three games, as Cal continued his rampage, hitting a series-leading .400.

The Orioles then moved into the World Series against the Philadelphia Phillies. Once again, they dropped the first game, but then they took out their broom and swept the Phils in four straight. It all came together for the Orioles in Game 5, as Scott McGregor pitched a shutout, while Eddie Murray poled a pair of home runs. But the golden moment for Cal and the Birds came when Garry Maddux hit a line drive right to shortstop. Cal caught the rocket that ended the game and crowned the Orioles as world champions!

Cal quickly had a second reason to celebrate when it was announced that he had been selected as the American League's Most Valuable Player. Ironically, Cal, who whacked 27 dingers while driving in 102 runs and hitting .318, just edged out his teammate and best friend, Eddie Murray, who had had a glorious season himself, with 33 home runs, 111 RBIs, and a .306 batting average.

Cal had led the AL in runs scored (121) and had led the majors in doubles (47), and had more hits (211) than had ever been recorded in a single season by any Hall of Fame shortstop.

But to Cal, winning the MVP Award and even a World Series wasn't everything. He had another goal in mind.

"I'd like to play every game, every inning, every day for twenty years," Cal said.

That's what Cal wanted more than anything—to play as well as he could for as long as he could.

4. A Family Affair

After only two full seasons in the majors, Cal had already achieved a lifetime's worth of dreams. He had gone from Rookie of the Year to MVP, while helping the Orioles win the World Series. But anyone who thought that he might rest on those laurels didn't know much about Cal Ripken. Cal wasn't interested in what he had already accomplished, but in what he had to do to improve his play.

Cal entered the new season determined to improve his fielding. He had made 25 errors in 1983 and he wanted to work hard to lower that number in 1984. Although Cal wasn't successful in cutting down on his miscues, he did throw out 583 base runners, a new record for assists by a shortstop in the American League. Cal also produced another big year at the plate, finishing with a .304 average and 27 home runs, topping all other major league shortstops. He was also third in the American League with 195 hits and third in extra-base hits, and drove in 86 runs.

But, despite Cal's efforts, the Orioles had an off year, finishing with an 85–77 record, and a fifth place finish in the AL East. When the Detroit Tigers beat the San Diego Padres in the World Series, Cal had to be content to watch the games on TV.

Early in the 1985 season, Cal had an ankle injury that threatened to sideline him and put an end to his consecutive game streak. On April 10, he caught a spike on top of second base and was sure he heard the ankle break. The X-rays taken after the game were negative, but the ankle was badly swollen. Still, Cal was back for the next game, playing through the pain. At the end of the 1985 season, his consecutive game streak stood at 603 games, a total of 5,455 innings. At the plate, Cal kept up his pace, hitting .282, with 26 homers and 110 RBI, astonishing power production for a shortstop.

Unfortunately, Cal's teammates couldn't keep up with him, and the O's limped to the finish line in fourth place, 16 games behind the division-winning Toronto Blue Jays.

The Orioles' mediocre play had prompted the team's general manager to fire Altobelli before the midpoint of the '85 season, and bring back Earl Weaver as manager. But Weaver hadn't been able to make the Birds fly high either, and they crash-landed the following season, finishing in last place for the first time since the franchise had moved to Baltimore in 1954.

Although Cal had had his usual productive year with the stick, and cut his errors down to 13, he would have gladly traded in his personal stats for a first-place finish by the team.

Cal was delighted, though, when the Orioles' front office finally decided to give his dad a shot at managing the Orioles for the 1987 season. The appointment made Cal and his father only the third father-son manager-player combination in major league history.

But the announcement did create questions in the minds of fans, players, and sportscasters. Would Ripken, Sr. be able to effectively manage his son? Would he play favorites? Or would he go in the opposite direction and be too hard on Cal?

In answer to these tough questions, Ripken, Sr. had just one thing to say: "In managing baseball, everyone becomes my son. You're everything to those kids. Now this young fellow comes along who happens to be my real son. Well, so what?... He knows my job and I know his. We're both professionals."

In July, the Birds called up Billy Ripken from the minors. For the baseball-loving Ripkens, it was like a dream come true, but some people saw the need to revisit the questions about fairness.

Cal answered those questions straight on. "From a family perspective it's pretty exciting. But it's no problem on the professional level. Dad taught us to approach it that way, because he always did. There's no favoritism. Some people may think that Billy is here because Dad is the manager, but that's not true. We all have a job to do."

To reinforce the image of fairness, Ripken, Sr. laid down an important rule. On the diamond, the boys didn't call their father "Dad" and he didn't call them "Son."

So it was that the brothers began playing side by side, Billy at second base, and Cal at shortstop. They practiced together, too, running wind sprints together and playing hockey with a ball and a bat in the locker room. The two competed against each other, but in a friendly way. And Billy knew he could learn a lot from his older brother.

"He's giving me All-Star advice. He's teaching me to do everything," Billy said.

But even with his brother and his dad at his side, Cal couldn't do enough to pull the Birds out of their downward spiral. Even though he led the team with 27 home runs and 98 RBIs, his batting average dipped to .252, while the Orioles dropped to a dismal 67–95 record.

Once again, Cal had played every single game, but his streak of playing every inning ended at a record of 8,243 consecutive innings when his dad pulled him out of a game in September, the first time that he had left a game since 1982.

It may have been a losing season on the field, but 1987 marked an important milestone for Cal in his personal life. Shortly after the season ended, Cal married Kelly Geer. He had proposed to her the previous New Year's Eve in a very romantic way. After dinner at his house, Cal had invited Kelly out on the balcony. There, in the yard, he had spelled out "Will You Marry Me?" in Christmas tree lights.

When they were married in November, Cal's dad served as best man, and brother Billy was an usher.

Actually life outside of baseball was a lot brighter for Cal than it was inside, especially after the Orioles opened the season with six straight losses and his father was demoted from manager to third base coach. The new field general was Frank

Robinson, a Hall of Fame outfielder who had played for the Orioles for six seasons starting in 1966.

But Robinson, who had helped lead the Birds to four pennants and a pair of World Series wins as a player, wasn't able to turn the team around as a manager. The Orioles finished the season as the divisional doormat at 54–107, the second worst record in the majors that year.

Cal felt awful about playing for a team that was constantly losing. "Nothing can be worse than this," he told reporters. "But we can learn from these bad times. No matter what happens in the future, we can say, 'We'll handle this. It can't be as bad as what happened in 1988.' We'll be stronger for it."

Baltimore fans were worried, though, that Cal might decide to become a free agent. They knew that he didn't like playing on a team that wasn't competitive, and they also knew that he had been hurt by his dad's demotion.

But Cal put all those rumors and concerns to rest when he signed a new contract with the Orioles that would pay him $2.45 million a year for three years, making him one of baseball's best-paid players.

"I started a job when I came here in 1981," Cal said. "The job is far from being finished. So I'm staying in Baltimore. I've got work to do."

Cal was committed not only to the Baltimore Orioles, but to the community itself. He made contributions to the Children's Center at Johns Hopkins Hospital. He also donated money to the School of Performing Arts in Baltimore. He bought tickets for underprivileged children and senior citizens for Orioles' home games. He and his wife Kelly even created their own foundation, a foundation dedicated to helping Baltimore-area adults learn to read and improve their math skills. And Cal was also involved in campaigns to motivate young people to stay healthy, to stay away from smoking, and to remain in school.

Cal also showed that his dedication to his fans as well. When a game was over, he often stayed several hours afterwards, signing autographs for every single fan that asked him. At one point, the Orioles' publicity director joked that Cal's streak would probably end "because of a wrist injury from signing so much."

But staying in Baltimore got that much tougher when it was announced that Eddie Murray, Cal's closest friend on the team, had been traded to the Dodgers. The parting was a bitter blow for both Cal and Eddie, who had come to count on each other in good times and bad.

The shakeup in the team had been so complete that by the time Cal arrived at spring training for the start of the new season, he was the only player remaining from the team that had won the 1983 World Series. Although it had only been six years since the Birds had hoisted the championship banner over Memorial Stadium, the horrible play of the recent Orioles' teams made people wonder if the glory days would ever return to Baltimore.

5. The Birds are Back

The Birds finally flew back towards the top in 1989. Although they couldn't quite nail down the divisional championship, they were contenders, finishing in second place, only two games behind the Blue Jays.

Cal, who slammed 21 home runs and 93 RBIs to spark the Orioles' resurgence, became the first shortstop in major league history to hit at least 20 round-trippers in eight straight seasons. Cal also compiled the best fielding percentage of any big-league shortstop in 1989, and was third in the voting for the AL MVP.

Cal also caused a stir by getting tossed out of a game by umpire Drew Coble. Although Cal is extremely competitive, he plays the game like a true professional and very rarely argues with umpires. "It felt like I was throwing God out of Sunday School," said Coble.

That fall, Cal once again found joy in his personal life when Kelly gave birth to their daughter, Rachel Marie, in November. And he was also thrilled to be the first winner of the Bart Giamatti Caring Award, which is given annually in honor of the late baseball commissioner. "Just as Bart Giamatti was a caring person, so is Cal Ripken, Jr.," said Ralph Branca in announcing the award. "Giamatti's devotion to baseball and education is mirrored in the things that Cal has done."

Cal, though, found himself involved in turmoil on the field after he got off to a slow start at the beginning of the 1990 season. Some fans, as well as some people in the media, suggested that Cal and the team would benefit if he took a day off every now and then. Even Baltimore's catcher, Rick Dempsey, suggested that a day off might help Cal.

"It will never happen," said Cal, who believes in playing every game that he is able to play. "I just look at the lineup card and take the field."

It wasn't that Cal simply ignored the suggestions that he might help the team by taking off a game or two. "There have been a couple of times that I thought, 'Would it really improve things if I gave into the criticism? I've tried everything else. Is taking a rest the only thing left to correct?'

"The most difficult part of the streak is when I'm struggling and I have to defend my desire to be in the lineup. But I never got to the point when taking a day off became a serious consideration. It would have seemed like running away."

Cal didn't take a day off, and on June 12 he reached a major career milestone when he moved past Everett Scott, who had played in 1,307 consecutive games. The only player who had compiled a longer streak than Cal's was the "Iron Horse," Hall of Famer Lou Gehrig, who had played in 2,130 straight games for the New York Yankees between June 1, 1925 and April 30, 1939.

Although Frank Robinson didn't bench Cal or insist that he take a game or two off to recapture his stroke, he did drop Cal and his .209 average from the third spot in the batting order to the sixth. Even a late-season surge only brought Cal's average up to .250, the lowest full-season average of his career.

Cal, as usual, did post decent power numbers, however, while leading the O's in nine offensive categories. And he was a virtual vacuum cleaner in the field, committing only three errors, an all-time record low for shortstops. Cal, who produced a .996 fielding percentage, had streaks of 96 errorless games and 431 chances without a miscue, both of which are also all-time marks for a shortstop.

During the offseason, Cal worked harder than ever on his hitting. He had a gym complete with a batting cage built into his new house, and he spent hours practicing his swing. Cal knew that to play every game, he would have to be in tremendous shape, so he developed a now-legendary workout routine. In addition to making diligent use of the batting cage, Cal also uses a tennis machine that shoots balls out at him so that he can practice his fielding. Then it's time to lift weights to tone and strengthen his muscles, before moving on to aerobic exercises that increase his stamina.

Cal also gets lots of exercise playing basketball with local kids. And his wife, Kelly, who was quite a basketball player herself in high school, will occasionally challenge him to a game of one-on-one.

But when it came to hitting, Cal once again found that he needed to go back to basics. He developed a new stance, crouching just slightly with his feet spread apart. And he changed his attitude about hitting. During the 1990 season, he had tried to make up for the poor hitting of his teammates by becoming overly aggressive, and had developed the bad habit of swinging at pitches that were out of the strike zone.

"I decided to wait for the ball instead of trying to hit it before it got to me," Cal said.

All of Cal's physical and mental work paid huge dividends in 1991, as he raised his game to a new level and turned in a season that most other players can only dream about. Cal started collecting his awards at the All-Star Game when he ran away from the competition in the pregame Home Run Derby by ripping 12 balls into the seats of Toronto's SkyDome, seven more than runner-up Paul O'Neill. "Every pitch looked big up there, like a beach ball," said Cal. "It was fun."

The following day Cal had some more good times when he set an American League record by starting in his eighth straight All-Star Game, and then went on to win the game's MVP award by smoking a three-run homer that powered the Junior Circuit to a 4–2 win over the National League.

But it was an event 10 days later that held even more meaning for Cal. At the beginning of his 1,500th consecutive game, he was presented with his All-Star MVP award, and he immediately announced that he was donating the van he had received as part of the award to the Cal Ripken, Jr. Learning

Center, the literacy program that he and Kelly developed for adults who had trouble reading. Cal made the game even more memorable by smacking his 20th home run of the season, the tenth straight year that he had achieved this feat.

"Without a doubt, this was a special night. I hold this night deep," said Cal.

Cal closed out the 1991 season with a .323 average, 34 home runs, and 114 RBIs, joining former Chicago Cubs star Ernie Banks as the only shortstop to ever hit .300, hammer 30 home runs, and drive in 100 runs in a single season. Defensively, he led all AL shortstops in putouts, assists, and fielding percentage, while earning his first Gold Glove as the top-fielding shortstop in the league.

Cal enjoyed still another special moment when his Gold Glove was presented by Mike Hirsh, a man who had recently graduated from the Ripken Learning Center.

"It was a storybook-type of season," said Cal, who won most of the major player honors, including the Sporting News and Associated Press Player of the Year awards, as well as being named the American League's MVP. "I just couldn't seem to do anything wrong. I guess it was just my year," added Cal, who joined Banks and another former Cubbie, Andre Dawson, as the only players to be named League MVP while performing on a team that had compiled less than a .500 record.

The only disappointing note in Cal's glittering season—other than the fact that he made the last out ever recorded in Memorial Stadium—was that his amazing performance couldn't stop the Birds from finishing at 67–95, the second worst record in the American League.

That shoddy performance by the O's, followed by a slow start in 1992, wound up causing another round of managerial musical chairs, with Johnny Oates replacing Frank Robinson in April.

Offensively, Cal didn't do much to help the Orioles get off to a flying start in their new home, the beautifully designed

Camden Yards. His batting average nosedived down to .251, his RBI total dipped to 72, and he managed to hit only 14 round-trippers, making it the first time that he had failed to hit more than 20 home runs in a full season. But Cal's slip with the stick didn't affect his slick fielding, which earned him his second straight Gold Glove.

Although Cal had what was for him a poor season on the field, the Orioles gave him a great big birthday present on August 24: a new five-year contract extension that paid Cal $30.5 million. Cal also won two awards in the offseason that showed that he's a Most Valuable Person as well as a Most Valuable Player.

Cal was named the 22nd winner of the Roberto Clemente Award, which is named after the Hall of Fame right fielder of the Pittsburgh Pirates, who died in a plane crash while attempting to deliver food and medicine to earthquake victims in Nicaragua. The award is given to the player who best represents the game, both on and off the field, with consideration given to sportsmanship, community involvement, and an individual's contribution to his team and to baseball.

Cal also received the Lou Gehrig Award, an annual honor that is given to the major leaguer who best represents the character of the former Yankee and Hall of Fame first baseman.

The 1993 season started on a sour note for Cal because both his father and brother had been cut loose by the Orioles. The twin releases left Cal feeling "weird and saddened and a little bit disoriented."

The situation wasn't helped any when the O's got off to a slow start. Then, in June, Cal sustained an injury that threatened his consecutive games streak. In an onfield fracas in a game against the Mariners, Cal's spikes caught in the grass. His knee stiffened up, and Cal didn't think he would be able to play the next day.

But once again, Cal fought through the pain and continued

his streak.

"I seriously thought I wasn't going to play," said Cal. "I was fine with it. And if something happens to break the streak, I would hope I'd be fine again. Having it taken away wouldn't affect my feeling for baseball, or my approach.

"I never set out to do this streak thing. I was raised with a work ethic, and an approach to baseball that said that the object of the game was to do whatever it takes to win.

"I'm proud of the streak for the fact that my teammates would rely on me being in the lineup. So the streak's just an extension of my approach, and my beliefs."

July, though, turned into a good month for Cal, both off and on the field. First, he became a father once again, this time to a son, Ryan Calvin. And on July 15, he hit his 278th homer to pass Ernie Banks as the top home run hitting shortstop in major league history.

The Orioles started heading in the right direction, finishing in a tie for third in the AL East. And Cal turned in his usual banner year at the plate, as he led major league shortstops in home runs for the ninth time in 11 seasons and in RBIs for the eighth time. Cal also sparkled in the field, leading AL shortstops in assists for a record-tying seventh season.

And with every game played, Cal was coming closer and closer to Lou Gehrig's record.

6. "One Moment in Time"

For baseball fans and players, 1994 turned out to be one of the most frustrating years ever. It was the season that baseball came to an early end. No playoffs, no World Series. The boys of summer went on strike in early August and the season came to a sudden halt.

The strike cut short the sensational record-threatening seasons that were being carved out by young superstars such as Ken Griffey, Jr. and Frank Thomas, as well as a serious bid by Tony Gwynn to become the first player to hit .400 since Ted Williams did the deed in 1941.

The work stoppage also closed down another big season by Cal, who was hitting .315, with 13 dingers—including the 300th of his career—and 75 RBIs in only 112 games. Just as importantly, however, the strike put Cal's pursuit of Lou Gehrig's consecutive games played streak on hold at 2,009 games, 131 behind the record that had been set by the "Iron Horse" in 1939.

In January, the executive council, the ruling body of Major League Baseball, made an important decision—if the strike didn't end in time for the start of the 1995 season, the teams would be permitted to use replacement players. The owners hoped the announcement would put pressure on the striking players to cave in to the owners' demands. But the players remained united, including Cal, who declared that he would support the union even if it meant sacrificing his consecutive game streak.

"Cal wants to make it clear that any individual achievement, recognition, or honors that he might receive are subordinate to his role as a union member," declared Cal's agent Ron Shapiro.

Cal's accomplishments on and off the field command such respect, however, that both the owners and the players agreed that if replacement players were used, Cal's streak would remain intact until the striking players returned.

The labor dispute was temporarily settled the following spring, and the 1995 season got underway, although two weeks later than usual. But by that time millions of fans had been turned off by this latest battle between the players and the owners, and there was a decided decline in interest as well as in attendance at the games.

Fortunately, Cal Ripken, Jr. and the values that he stands for were around to provide some much-needed luster to the tarnished sport.

Although Cal always liked to play at a pace of one game at a time, and to not even talk about the streak or think about breaking Gehrig's record, he realized as far back as spring training that 1995 couldn't be a typical year for him.

"I'm trying very hard to look at this like a regular season, but I'm already having a difficult time trying to do that," said Cal.

As the spring turned into summer, the tension kept mounting as Cal moved relentlessly towards the standard that had been set by Gehrig 56 years earlier. Then, on September 5, Cal finally tied Gehrig's astonishing record. With the hometown Orioles holding a 7–0 lead over the California Angels, the game became official as soon as the Angels made their third out of the fifth inning. And at that exact moment, the huge orange and black banners that were hanging on the warehouse that overlooks Camden Yards' right field wall were changed, like an old-time scoreboard, from 2–1–2–9 to 2–1–3–0.

That was the same moment that the 46,804 fans who filled Camden Yards rose to give Cal a standing ovation that lasted for more than five minutes. Cal also had them on their feet and cheering in the sixth inning, when he cracked a homer, his 14th of the year, into the left field bleachers. And everyone went home happy as the Birds beat the Angels, 8–0.

"Honestly, it's not something that I set out to do," said Cal.

"I don't compare myself to Lou Gehrig. The only thing we might have in common is a great desire to play…. He's one of the greatest baseball players that ever played. I am not and never will be," added Cal with sincere but perhaps misplaced modesty.

The scale of what Cal accomplished can be seen in the fact that the player who was closest to Cal's consecutive game streak was Frank Thomas, whose total stood at a mere 235 games. And in the entire history of the sport, only six players have ever compiled a streak of more than 1,000 games.

The following day, September 6, started out as a routine day for Cal when he drove his five-year-old daughter Rachel to her first day of kindergarten. But that was just the calm before the storm of one of the most extraordinary days in baseball history.

Thousands of excited fans lined up at the gates of Camden Yards hours before the turnstiles were even scheduled to open. And among the overflowing crowd that finally settled in their seats were President Bill Clinton and his daughter, Chelsea, Vice President Al Gore, Frank Robinson, and Brooks Robinson. Other Hall of Famers, such as former Chicago Cubs shortstop Ernie Banks and the Yankee Clipper, Joe DiMaggio, were also there, as well as jazz saxophonist and composer Branford Marsalis, who along with Bruce Hornsby, played the national anthem.

Then the evening's festivities got started as Cal's two children Rachel and Ryan tossed ceremonial first balls to their dad. Cal added to the theatrical atmosphere in storybook fashion by ripping a fourth inning rope over the left field fence that upped the Orioles' lead to 3–1 over the Angels.

After Orioles' starter Mike Mussina set the Angels down in the top of the fifth inning, a joyous bedlam broke out in the stadium as the orange and black banners gave graphic evidence to the fact that Cal had played in his 2,131st consecutive game, the longest streak in baseball history.

The historic moment, which occurred at precisely 9:20:09 Eastern Daylight Time, also touched off a fireworks display as well as a torrent of orange and black balloons and streamers, while loudspeakers blared the song, "One Moment in Time." More thrilling, though, was the standing ovation that went on for over 22 minutes while fans kept yelling, "We want Cal!" Although he left the dugout to take six curtain calls, the fans still hadn't had enough, so halfway through the demonstration of affection that was raining down, two of Cal's teammates pushed him out of the dugout and he proceeded to take a victory lap all around the field, high-fiving and shaking the hands of his fans, the umpires, and then stopping at the Angels' dugout, where he shook hands with the California players.

Then Cal walked over to the box seats where his family was gathered, and handed them his game jersey. Underneath, he wore a T-shirt that read:

2,130 + Hugs and Kisses For Daddy

Then Cal wiped his hands on his pants, mouthed to the crowd, "No more" and got ready to play once again. After all, this was Cal Ripken, and for Cal the idea has always been to just play ball.

In the celebration after the game, Joe DiMaggio, who had been Lou Gehrig's teammate, took the time to remember Gehrig as well as to congratulate Cal. "There's a beautiful monument to Lou Gehrig at Yankee Stadium that says, 'A man, a gentleman, and a great ballplayer whose amazing record of 2,130 games should stand for all time.' That goes to prove that even the greatest records are made to be broken.

"And wherever my former teammate is today, I'm sure he's tipping his cap off to you, Cal Ripken."

Gehrig's career had been cut short in 1939 by an illness that would cause his death only two years later. To date, there is no cure for the malady that now goes by the name Lou Gehrig's disease. So Cal honored Gehrig in the best way that he could by presenting a check for more than a million dollars to Johns Hopkins Hospital for the purpose of establishing a foundation that will be dedicated to finding a cure for the disease. The money for the check had been collected from ticket sales for special field seats that had been erected especially to handle the overflow crowd of fans who had wanted to see Cal set the record.

As the closing ceremonies continued, one speaker after another honored Gehrig and praised Cal for all that he has done, not only to earn the "Iron Man" nickname, but for what he has contributed to his team and to the city of Baltimore, and for being a loving family member.

During one emotional moment, Mark Belanger, the player that Cal had looked up to as a kid, presented him with a hard hat and announced that a new ballfield would be built in Aberdeen so that kids in the area would have a safe place to play ball.

When it came time for Cal to speak, he began by thanking the people who had supported him. He started with his fans first. "I want to make sure that you know how I feel," he said. "As I grew up here, I not only had dreams of being a big-league ballplayer, but also of being a Baltimore Oriole. I thank you, the fans of Baltimore, from the bottom of my heart. This is the greatest place to play."

Then he went on to thank four special people in his life. First, he acknowledged his father, who taught him to "play the right way and to play the Oriole way.... From the very beginning, my dad let me know how important it was to be there for your team, and to be counted on by your teammates."

Then, turning to his mom, who had taught him so much about the game, he said, "She let my Dad lead the way on the field but she was there in every other way, leading and shaping the family. She's always been my inspiration."

And then he went on to talk about his early experience with the Orioles. "When I got to the big leagues there was a man, Eddie Murray, who showed me how to play this game day in and day out. I thank him for his example and his friendship. I was lucky to have him as my teammate for the years that we were together, and I congratulate him on his record of 3,000 hits this year."

Finally, he turned to his wife Kelly and spoke of his love for her and for their children. "She has enriched [my life] with her friendship and her love." Looking at her, he said, "You, Rachel, and Ryan are my life."

Finally, Cal spoke his simple closing words, which brought tears to most of the 46,272 fans that crammed Camden Yards as well as a national television audience.

"I know that if Lou Gehrig is looking down on tonight's activities, he isn't concerned about someone playing one more consecutive game than he did. Instead, he's viewing tonight as just another example of what is good and right about the great game of baseball.

"Whether your name is Gehrig or Ripken, DiMaggio or Robinson, or that of some youngster who picks up his bat or puts on his glove, you are challenged by the game of baseball to do your best, day in and day out, and that's all I've ever tried to do."

Cal has met that challenge game after game for 2,153 consecutive contests and counting, as he gets ready for the 1996 season. As far as the streak is concerned, no one can predict when it may end, but it's pretty certain that Cal is not going to sit himself down. And as Phil Regan, who took over as the O's manager in 1995 noted, "When he's 38 or 39, he may want to take a day off, but I'm not going to take him out of the lineup." And Davey Johnson, who was named the Orioles' manager for 1996, isn't likely to leave Cal's name off the lineup card, either.

Certainly, Cal's streak is an absolutely awesome achievement, especially when it is put in some perspective. For example, while Cal was playing in every game for 14-plus seasons, 3,717 players went on the disabled list, and the other 27 teams used a combined total of 520 starting shortstops.

The streak will undoubtedly be recalled as Cal's greatest achievement. But that astonishing accomplishment shouldn't obscure the fact that Cal has been a consistent superstar as well as the most physically dependable player in the history of the sport.

He has set or shares 12 major league or American League fielding records, and has also set a number of all-time hitting records for shortstops. And in addition to his Rookie of the Year Award and his pair of MVP plaques, Cal has played in 13 consecutive All-Star Games, yet another AL record for short-stops.

Cal has, without question, already established himself as a future Hall of Famer, and just as importantly he has earned the gratitude of his other "team," the citizens of the city of Baltimore.

As both a player and as a person, Calvin Edwin Ripken, Jr. has not only stood up to the challenges, but has gone on to set standards that honor him and the game of baseball.

Dear Reader,

One of the nicest rewards of being an author is receiving some very wonderful letters from readers. And while I don't want to discourage any writers, I thought I would use this page to answer the most asked questions that come in the mail.

I was born on November 14, 1941 in Brooklyn, which is one of the five boroughs that comprise New York City. I grew up on Ocean Parkway, and I spent most of the time through my teenage years playing one sport or another. In looking back, I wish I had spent some of that time reading some of the wonderful books that I later discovered by reading them with my children.

I'm not exactly sure why I became a writer, but I know that part of the reason is that I have a passion to communicate and create-whether I'm writing a book, baking a loaf of bread, or growing a flower or a broccoli. I've always enjoyed working with my hands, bringing something into life and sharing my ideas and feelings with other people.

I'm sure that another reason has to do with four wonderful teachers that I was fortunate enough to have when I was growing up. The first was my mother, Betty, who taught me the joy of music and to take life's bumps with a smile (she did it better than I do it) and to keep moving forward. She also taught me, as Martin Luther King, Jr., would try to teach the world, to judge people by the contents of their characters and their deeds, and not by the superficialities of skin color, their current or past country of origin, or their religious beliefs (or their lack of those beliefs.)

Then there was Katherine Lynch-a teacher of history and so much more-whose path I was so lucky to cross when I decided to spend my 10th grade in Silver Spring, Maryland. After all these years I still can't express just how much she gave me. Then came Malcolm Largman, my 11th grade English teacher at Lafayette High School, the first person to give me the notion and the confidence that I could become a writer.

Finally, there was Jackie Robinson, a great baseball player and phenomenal human being whose example taught me how to walk alone when I had to, and to confront ignorance and bigotry not with physical weapons or hatred, but with courage and dignity.

To all my teachers-past, present, and future-thank you!

Richard J. Brenner

If you want to write to the author, address your letter to:

Richard J. Brenner
c/o East End Publishing
54 Alexander Dr.
Syosset NY 11791

Please note that letters *will not* be answered unless they include a self-addressed stamped envelope.

If you want to write to the players, address your letters to:

Greg Maddux
Atlanta Baseball Team
Atlanta Fulton-County Stadium
PO Box 4064
Atlanta GA 30302-4064

Cal Ripken, Jr.
Baltimore Orioles
333 W. Camden St.
Baltimore MD 21201

If you want to write a letter complaining about team nicknames and logos, you may write to individual teams and/or to the commissioners. Or better yet, start a petition drive in your school or neighborhood.

Here are some addresses:

Baseball Commissioner's Office
Major League Baseball
350 Park Avenue
NY NY 10022

Commissioner Pete Tagliabue
c/o NFL
410 Park Avenue
NY NY 10022

Cleveland Baseball Team
Jacobs Field
2401 Ontario Street
Cleveland OH 44115

Washington NFL Football Team
21300 Redskin Park Drive
Ashburn VA 22011

Sources

Atlanta Constitution

Baltimore Sun

Baseball Digest

Cal Ripken, Junior by Glen Macnow

Cal Ripken, Junior: Oriole Ironman by Stew Thornley

Cal Ripken: Quiet Hero by Lois Nicholson

Cal Ripken: Star Shortstop by Jeff Savage

Chicago Tribune

Columbus Dispatch

Gentleman's Quarterly

New York Times

Sport

The Sporting News

Sports Illustrated

Sports Illustrated for Kids

USA Today Baseball Weekly

GREG MADDUX

Birthdate: April 14, 1966 **Birthplace:** San Angelo, Texas

Height: 6-0 **Weight:** 175

Bats: R **Throws:** R

Career Record

Year	Club	W-L	ERA	G	GS	CG	SHO	SV	IP	H	R	ER	BB	SO
1984	Pikeville	6-2	2.63	14	12	2	2	0	85.2	63	35	25	41	62
1985	Peoria	13-9	3.19	27	27	6	0	0	186.0	176	86	66	52	125
1986	Pittsfield	4-3	2.69	8	4	2	0	0	63.2	49	19	19	35	35
	Iowa	10-1	3.02	18	18	5	2	0	128.1	127	49	43	30	65
	Chicago	2-4	5.52	6	5	1	0	0	31.0	44	20	19	11	20
1987	Iowa	3-1	0.98	4	4	2	2	0	27.2	17	3	3	12	22
	Chicago	6-14	5.61	30	27	1	1	0	155.2	181	111	97	74	101
1988	Chicago	18-8	3.18	34	34	9	3	0	249.0	230	97	88	81	140
1989	Chicago	19-12	2.95	35	35	7	1	0	238.1	222	90	78	82	135
1990	Chicago	15-15	3.46	35	35	8	2	0	237.0	242	116	91	71	144
1991	Chicago	15-11	3.35	37	37	7	2	0	263.0	232	113	98	66	198
1992	Chicago	20-11	2.18	35	35	9	4	0	268.0	201	68	65	70	199
1993	Atlanta	20-10	2.36	36	36	8	1	0	267.0	228	85	70	52	197
1994	Atlanta	16-6	1.56	25	25	10	3	0	202.0	150	44	35	31	156
1995	Atlanta	19-2	1.63	28	28	10	3	0	209.2	147	39	38	23	181
Minor Totals		36-15	2.86	83	19	8	0	491.1	195	156	150	309		
M.L. Totals		150-93	2.88	297	70	20	0	2,120.2	1,877	679	561	1,471		
Atlanta Totals		55-18	1.90	89	28	7	0	678.2	525	143	106	534		

League Championship Series Record

Year	Club/Opp	W-L	ERA	G	GS	CG	SHO	IP	H	R	ER	BB	SO
1989	Chi vs. SF	0-1	13.50	2	2	0	0	7.1	13	12	11	4	5
1993	Atl vs. Phi	1-1	4.97	2	2	0	0	12.2	11	8	7	7	11

CALVIN EDWARD RIPKEN, JR.

Birthdate: August 24, 1960 **Birthplace:** Havre de Grace, Maryland

Height: 6'4" **Weight:** 220

Bats: R **Throws:** R

Year	AVG	G	AB	R	H	2B	3B	HR	RBI	BB	SO	SB	CS
1981	.128	23	39	1	5	0	0	0	0	1	8	0	0
1982	.264	160	598	90	158	32	5	28	93	46	95	3	3
1983	.318	+162	*663	*121	*211	*47	2	27	102	58	97	0	4
1984	.304	+162	641	103	195	37	7	27	86	71	89	2	1
1985	.282	161	642	116	181	32	5	26	110	67	68	2	3
1986	.282	162	627	98	177	35	1	25	81	70	60	4	2
1987	.252	*162	624	97	157	28	3	27	98	81	77	3	5
1988	.264	161	575	87	152	25	1	23	81	102	69	2	2
1989	.257	+162	646	80	166	30	0	21	93	57	72	3	2
1990	.250	161	600	78	150	28	4	21	84	82	66	3	1
1991	.323	+162	650	99	210	46	5	34	114	53	46	6	1
1992	.251	*162	637	73	160	29	1	14	72	64	50	4	3
1993	.257	*162	*641	87	165	26	3	24	90	65	58	1	4
1994	.315	112	444	71	140	19	3	13	75	32	41	1	0
1995	.262	144	550	71	144	33	2	17	88	52	59	0	1
M.L. TOTALS	.276	2,218	8,577	1,272	2,371	447	42	327	1,267	901	955	34	32

* - Led League + - Tied for League Lead

	AVG	G	AB	R	H	2B	3B	HR	RBI	BB	SO	SB	CS
ALCS 1983	.400	4	15	5	6	2	0	0	1	2	3	0	0
WS 1983	.167	5	18	2	3	0	0	0	1	3	4	0	0

If you enjoyed this book, you might want to order some of our other exciting titles:

BASKETBALL SUPERSTARS ALBUM 1996, Richard J. Brenner. Includes 16 full-color pages, and mini-bios of the game's top superstars, plus career and all-time stats. 48 pages.

MICHAEL JORDAN * MAGIC JOHNSON, by Richard J. Brenner. A dual biography of two of the greatest superstars of all time. 128 pages, 15 dynamite photos.

ANFERNEE HARDAWAY * GRANT HILL, by Brian Cazeneuve. A dual biography of two of the brightest young stars in basketball. 96 pages, 10 pages of photos.

SHAQUILLE O'NEAL * LARRY JOHNSON, by Richard J. Brenner. A dual biography of two of the brightest young stars in basketball. 96 pages, 10 pages of photos.

STEVE YOUNG * JERRY RICE, by Richard J. Brenner. A dual biography of the two superstars who led the 49ers to the Super Bowl. 96 pages, 10 pages of photos.

TROY AIKMAN * STEVE YOUNG, by Richard J. Brenner. A dual biography of the top two quarterbacks in the NFL. 96 pages, 10 pages of photos.

GREG MADDUX * CAL RIPKEN, JR., by Richard J. Brenner. A dual biography of two future Hall of Famers. 96 pages, 10 pages of photos.

KEN GRIFFEY JR. * FRANK THOMAS, by Brian Cazeneuve. A dual biography of two of baseball's brightest young superstars. 96 pages, 10 pages of photos.

BARRY BONDS * ROBERTO ALOMAR, by Bob Woods. A dual biography of two of the brightest stars in baseball. 96 pages, 10 pages of photos.

MARIO LEMIEUX, by Richard J. Brenner. An exciting biography of one of hockey's all-time greats. 96 pages, 10 pages of photos.

THE WORLD SERIES, THE GREAT CONTESTS, by Richard J. Brenner. The special excitement of the Fall Classic is brought to life through seven of the most thrilling Series ever played, including 1993. 176 pages, including 16 action-packed photos.

THE COMPLETE SUPER BOWL STORY, GAMES I-XXVIII, by Richard J. Brenner. The most spectacular moments in Super Bowl history are brought to life, game by game. 224 pages, including 16 memorable photos.

MICHAEL JORDAN, by Richard J. Brenner. An easy-to-read, photo-filled biography especially for younger readers. 32 pages.

SHAQUILLE O'NEAL, by Richard J. Brenner. An easy-to-read, photo-filled biography especially for younger readers. 32 pages.

WAYNE GRETZKY, by Richard J. Brenner. An easy-to-read, photo-filled biography especially for younger readers. 32 pages.

TOUCHDOWN! THE FOOTBALL FUN BOOK, by Richard J. Brenner. Trivia, puzzles, mazes and much more! 64 pages.

PLEASE SEE NEXT PAGE FOR ORDER FORM

ORDER FORM

Payment must accompany all orders and must be in U.S. dollars.

Postage and handling is $1.35 per book up to a maximum of $6.75 ($1.75 to a maximum of $8.75 in Canada).

Mr. Brenner will personally autograph his books for an additional cost of $1.00 per book.

Please send me the following books:

No. of copies	Title	Price
_____	BASKETBALL SUPERSTARS ALBUM 1996	$4.50/$6.25 Can.
_____	MICHAEL JORDAN * MAGIC JOHNSON	$3.50/$4.25 Can.
_____	ANFERNEE HARDAWAY * GRANT HILL	$3.99/$5.50 Can.
_____	SHAQUILLE O'NEAL * LARRY JOHNSON	$3.50/$4.50 Can.
_____	STEVE YOUNG * JERRY RICE	$3.99/$5.50 Can.
_____	TROY AIKMAN * STEVE YOUNG	$3.50/$4.50 Can.
_____	GREG MADDUX * CAL RIPKEN, JR.	$3.99/$5.50 Can.
_____	KEN GRIFFEY JR. * FRANK THOMAS	$3.50/$4.50 Can.
_____	BARRY BONDS * ROBERTO ALOMAR	$3.50/$4.50 Can.
_____	MARIO LEMIEUX	$3.50/$4.50 Can.
_____	THE WORLD SERIES, THE GREAT CONTESTS	$3.50/$4.50 Can.
_____	THE COMPLETE SUPER BOWL STORY GAMES I-XXVIII	$4.00/$5.00 Can.
_____	MICHAEL JORDAN	$4.00/$5.50 Can.
_____	SHAQUILLE O'NEAL	$3.25/$4.50 Can.
_____	WAYNE GRETZKY	$3.25/$4.50 Can.
_____	TOUCHDOWN! THE FOOTBALL FUN BOOK	$3.50/$5.00 Can.

TOTAL NUMBER OF BOOKS ORDERED   _____

TOTAL PRICE OF BOOKS $_____

POSTAGE AND HANDLING $_____

AUTOGRAPHING COST $_____

TOTAL PAYMENT ENCLOSED $_____

NAME _____

ADDRESS _____

CITY _____ STATE _____ ZIP _____ COUNTRY _____

Send to: East End Publishing, 54 Alexander Drive, Syosset NY 11791 USA. Dept. TD. Allow three weeks for delivery. Discounts are available on orders of 25 or more copies. For details call (516) 364-6383.